Stra

Ancient World

Strange Superstitions and Curious Customs of the Ancient World

Alicia Chrysostomou
&
Matheos Chrysostomou

MERCIER PRESS

MERCIER PRESS
Douglas Village, Cork
www.mercierpress.ie

Trade enquiries to CMD Distribution,
55a Spruce Avenue, Stillorgan Industrial Park, Blackrock, Dublin

ISBN 1 85635 494 6

10 9 8 7 6 5 4 3 2 1

Mercier Press receives financial assistance from
the Arts Council/An Chomhairle Ealaíon

Printed in Ireland by ColourBooks Ltd

Contents

Introduction

This book is a collection of the oddest, most eccentric, and at times truly bizarre, customs, laws and superstitions of our fore-fathers. While most of these accounts are taken from chronicles by the earliest known historians and geographers living in the Greece and Rome of old (the most 'modern' are taken from the medieval chronicles of Marco Polo), some also come from more recent discoveries of ancient ways of life. These diverse sources combine to create a comparative anthropology.

Many of the traditions related here seem surreal in these modern times. Some give an insight into the intensity with which our predecessors relied on their religious beliefs and rituals for guidance in their daily life, while others derive from super-stition and observation of nature. Amazingly some of these customs appear to have transcended the millennia and crop up extant as lore recognisable even today. It must be said however, that some of the extinct customs and laws seem quite sensible even by modern thinking and may be due for a re-introduction into today's society!

This collection of anecdotes refers mostly to peoples and civilisations long since gone. Some of the more powerful ancient nations have transcended the ages, remaining familiar to us from the pages of current geography books as well as the history books, but many have given way to successive civilisations many years ago and have left few traces of their existence.

1. Birth to the Grave

Conception:
The signs of imminent fertility in a woman, according to the Romans, were to be deduced from her eyes. Finding traces of medication in a woman's saliva, after its initial application to her eyes, was taken as an indication that she was ready to conceive.

❖   ❖   ❖

Through the Dark Ages conception was not permitted on a Sunday, Wednesday, Friday, during Lent or during Advent.

❖   ❖   ❖

Pregnancy:
Women eating overly salty food while pregnant were said by the Romans to give birth to babies without nails.

❖   ❖   ❖

A woman in medieval England who died while pregnant was not permitted a burial on consecrated ground as the child she was carrying was not baptised and so invalidated her rights to a Christian burial.

❖   ❖   ❖

Eagles in ancient Rome were observed to carry stones into their nests. These stones were thought to possess magical properties, for example, they were thought to be an effective means of preventing miscarriages.

❖   ❖   ❖

Birth:

Following a birth, the Trausi, a tribe living in ancient Thrace, would gather their family around the newborn. A common ritual perhaps, except the Trausi greeted the birth of a child with grief and tears. The assembled family would lament together over the sufferings and great sadness the child must endure now that it was born into the world. They would take great pains to point out just what miseries and trials must be faced through its life. Contrarily, once a family member had died, he was buried by his friends and relations amid whoops of joy. They would stand at the graveside and rejoice that death had brought their dearly departed an escape from the wretchedness that must otherwise be confronted on earth.

It was believed in ancient Greece that sitting with crossed legs or with fingers intertwined at the bedside of a woman giving birth would make her labour more difficult. Another magical charm causing the same result involved tying knots in the presence of the woman.

The Zar-dandan people, encountered by Marco Polo on his travels, inhabited an eastern province south of Tibet. When a Zar-dandan woman gave birth she was expected to immediately rise from her delivery, wash and clothe the baby then hand it over to her husband who would promptly take himself and the child off to the marital bed. He would remain there for forty days, rising only to answer calls of nature. During this period the husband would be visited by all his friends and relations who would spend their time trying to entertain him and cheer him up. The reasoning behind this unusual behaviour was to spare the wife the burden of having to tend to the baby as she had already had the trouble of carrying it for the duration of her pregnancy. She was not however spared from the burden of completing all the household work and waiting hand and foot on her husband as he lay in bed for his period of confinement.

The Manzi kingdom of the Middle Ages occupied a large section of eastern Asia. As soon as a Manzi child was born, its mother or father would make an exact note of the time, date, and astrological sign under which it was born. Then, armed with these details, the children would grow up with all the information needed to make decisions in life. So for instance if they wished to make a journey, they would pay a visit to the astrologer who would advise for or against the endeavour. Likewise, when a couple wished to marry, they would consult with the astrologer to learn if they were compatible and whether the match was written in the stars.

❖   ❖   ❖

Medieval women had to adhere to certain strict conditions following the birth of their children. A woman was not permitted to enter a church until thirty-three days had elapsed from the birth of a son or sixty-six days from the birth of a daughter. As the afterbirth was thought to attract demons, any woman dying before being allowed to re-enter the church was not permitted burial on consecrated ground.

❖   ❖   ❖

The Tlingits, a native Alaskan people, believed that a birth should not occur in the family house. To accommodate the mother-to-be, a hole would be dug at the back of the house with a crude shelter constructed over it. When the time came to give birth the woman was expected to retire to this hut no matter how inclement the weather.

❖   ❖   ❖

Following the birth of a child in ancient Greece the house door would be painted with pitch to keep away evil spirits. Items would also be hung outside the door, the nature of which depended on whether the child was a girl or boy. A wreath of olive branches would be hung for a boy and a fillet of wool for

11

a girl. On the sixth day following the birth, the father would decide whether to keep the child or to expose it. He would undergo a rite that involved him running naked around the family hearth with the child in his arms.

❖   ❖   ❖

Offspring:

Persian men had a goal in life: they took as many wives and mistresses as feasible with the sole aim of fathering as many children as possible. Their hope was to win the prizes promised by their king to those siring the most children.

❖   ❖   ❖

The Egyptians believed that a child was indebted to its father for its existence. For this reason all children born to a man had equal rights on his estate whether they were legitimate or not.

❖   ❖   ❖

A tribe of Libyans called the Psylli had a method of determining the legitimacy of a child when the mother was suspected of having an affair. The child would be placed in a bath with a sand viper. If the child touched the snake and the snake subsequently wilted it was taken as a sign that the child was legitimate.

❖   ❖   ❖

The Amazons and Gargarians were two tribes living adjacent to each other. The Amazons were a tribe consisting only of women and the Gargarians only of men. These two tribes lived independently of each other for ten months of the year, however for two months they would meet in an area bordering their territories. There they would sleep randomly with each other taking no particular partner, their aim solely being to make the women pregnant. Any children subsequently born of this fraternisation would be divided up with the females remaining with the Amazons, and the boys given to the Gargarians. Each Gargarian given a child to raise would adopt it as his own, irrespective of the true paternity of the child. Due to the conditions of conception, he had no idea if it did actually belong to him. The female babies retained by the Amazons had their right breasts seared so as to be better able to handle a bow and a javelin in later life.

❖   ❖   ❖

An ancient Libyan tribe called the Auses regarded women as common property with no married couples pairing off together. Because of this, the paternity of any child was uncertain. So, when a tribal child grew up, the men would hold a meeting to determine which of them this child most closely resembled. The man looking most like the child was deemed to be the father.

❖   ❖   ❖

A particular Indian tribe also held the policy of not pairing off and marrying. Instead, the children born to this tribe were considered as belonging to all. They were passed from nurse to nurse once they were born so that even their own mothers could not tell them apart. This policy was devised to foster a community spirit and prevent rivalry or civic disorder.

❖   ❖   ❖

In order to legitimise an illegitimate child, a Roman father would legally adopt the child. This liberal act would placate his concubine and ensure her faithfulness.

❖   ❖   ❖

The sponsor of a child in medieval Ireland stood for his godchild at baptism and promised also to become a gossip for the parents.

This later duty was thought to foster a mutual regard and friendship between the families.

❖   ❖   ❖

Circumcision:
The practice of circumcision predates even the oldest of current religious customs. Apparently, at one time Jews lived in an area between Syria and Arabia, then colonised by the Egyptians. The Egyptians already practised circumcision and as the Jews mingled with them, they took up the practice.

❖   ❖   ❖

Old Age:
The Albanians of ancient times were very respectful towards those of advanced age. Their courtesy extended also to the dead. Indeed the Albanians believed it was most impious to be at all concerned about a person once they were dead, so out of respect, they never again mentioned a person once they had passed away.

❖   ❖   ❖

Signs of Death:
The signs of impending death were listed for the Romans by their compatriot Pliny the Elder. Apparently, the signs to be watched for were; madness, laughter, disorder of the mind, playing with fringes and making folds in a bedspread. Unsurprisingly, also included in this list was taking no notice of a person trying to wake one! But the unmistakable signs were given by the appearance of the eyes and nostrils and continually lying on one's back.

❖   ❖   ❖

The Roman physician Celsus diagnosed imminent death as; when the patient lies on his back with his knees bent; when he keeps slipping down towards the foot of the bed; when he uncovers his arms and legs and tosses them about; when he gapes, and when he continually falls asleep.

❖ ❖ ❖

Death:

Scythia was a region spanning the north and north-east of the Black Sea during the classical era. When a Scythian died his nearest and dearest would put the body into a cart and set off on a round of visits to friends. At each friend's house the cortege would be invited in and have a meal served out to all in the party – including the corpse! After a forty-day trip around the neighbours' houses, the corpse would finally be buried.

❖ ❖ ❖

There was not much peace for a dying Libyan. Those gathered around a Libyan deathbed, seeing their friend or relation was about to breathe his last, would ensure their compatriot was sitting upright before passing into the next world. A Libyan would not under any circumstances allow anyone to die lying flat on their back. This same peculiarity extended after death also as Libyans were always buried in a seated position.

❖ ❖ ❖

Pity those hitting seventy in ancient Caspian society. Anyone reaching this ripe age would be starved to death and their body left on a brier in the desert. Their kinsfolk would stand watching at a distance, having deposited the corpse, to see what happened to the body. Should a bird come and take the body it was considered lucky. An animal, such as a dog, dragging the body off was thought a little less lucky, but if the body was left untouched it was considered to augur very bad luck.

❖ ❖ ❖

The Derbices, like their Black Sea neighbours the Caspians, also slaughtered their men folk once they reached the age of seventy. The body in this instance would be consumed by its closest relatives. Women were not permitted to live beyond seventy either, however they were dispatched by strangulation and then given a burial. Men who happened to die before reaching seventy, that is before their relatives had the chance to kill them, were not eaten on death but were, like the women, buried.

❖   ❖   ❖

A law of the Ceian, a people living in ancient Greece, stated that he who was not able to live well should not be required to live wretchedly. So, in accordance with this law, the Ceians had a policy of ordering all its citizens over sixty years of age to drink hemlock. This ensured that there would be sufficient food in the country for the rest of the citizens. In times of trouble, such as when their city was under siege, the age limit was reduced accordingly.

❖   ❖   ❖

The Bactrians, a tribe of ancient Persia, treated their old and infirm ruthlessly. Anyone who, through age or sickness, found they could no longer look after themselves were literally thrown out to the dogs. They would be cast out into the open and packs of dogs called 'the under-takers', which were specially kept for the purpose, would be set on them.

❖   ❖   ❖

The ancient Persian tribe of the Massagetae considered the best death to occur naturally in old age when their body would be chopped up with a portion of beef and eaten. However, those unlucky enough to succumb to disease were regarded as impious and thrown to the wild animals to eat.

Roman citizens would close the eyes of the dying as they felt it was not right for anyone to look into another's eyes at the moment of death. However, they would then make sure the eyes were open before the body was set on its funeral pyre to ensure they would be open towards heaven.

❖   ❖   ❖

The Hyperboreans were an ancient tribe believed to live beyond the north wind. They had a peculiar approach to death. They lived life to the full, then when they considered it was time for them to go, they set up a luxurious banquet. Having eaten their fill, they would leap into the sea to their death.

❖   ❖   ❖

The Yogi in the kingdom of Maabar situated in medieval India were very careful not to do anything which would cause hurt or pain to any other living creature. They were particularly careful of worms and went to extreme measures not to be the cause of breeding worms which would ultimately die, leaving the responsibility of their souls on the person concerned. For this reason they would cremate their dead so as not to leave any substance that may cause a worm to be generated. Similarly, when they relieved themselves they would break up all solid matter and disperse of it in such a way as to make the formation of worms difficult.

❖   ❖   ❖

Some Ethiopians of olden times encased their dead in coffins which they subsequently kept in their homes. They then used their dead to make oaths by invoking them as witnesses. These oaths were considered the most sacred of all.

❖   ❖   ❖

The closest relative of a dying Roman would ensure he inhaled the last breath of the dying man as this was thought to ensure the continuity of family life.

❖   ❖   ❖

A tribe of Native Americans known as the Seminoles would hold a new born baby over the face of its mother if the mother had died in childbirth. This act allowed the baby to receive the parting spirit of its mother.

❖   ❖   ❖

The Mesopotamians would always wash themselves having touched a corpse. They mourned their dead, unlike some societies of the era, and would bury them in honey, having first smeared wax over the body.

❖   ❖   ❖

The Egyptians abhorred anyone causing injury to or otherwise wounding any human. This attitude caused difficulties for those employed in the mummification industry, particularly those whose specific task it was to incise the corpse in preparation for the removal of its organs. As soon as he completed his task, this unlucky tradesman would have to take to his heels and run as anyone present would immediately stone him.

❖   ❖   ❖

If a Persian was falsely reported as having died while travelling away from home, they would not be allowed back in through their front door on returning home. Instead, a ritual would be observed whereby the traveller would have to be lowered into the house through a specially made hole in the roof. The traveller would then go through a period of time when they would be treated as a newborn baby.

The Greeks believed that death made a house impure. For this reason a warning branch would be set at the front door to alert any passer-by that a death had occurred in the house. Certain rituals were then performed to cleanse the house. If a fire was burning at the time of death, this was allowed to go out as it was thought to have become contaminated. The fire could only be re-lit once the house had been thoroughly swept. A bowl of water had to be provided by the door for any mourners coming to pay their last respects. They needed the water to wash themselves before returning to the street. The corpse was also placed in a particular position. It would always be placed with its feet facing the door so that it would know how to find its way out of the house, but not back in.

❖   ❖   ❖

The burial custom of the Baliares, now known more familiarly as the Balearics, involved dismembering a corpse with wooden knives, placing the pieces into jars and piling these onto a mound of stones.

❖   ❖   ❖

Suicide:
Unlike other societies, the philosophers of India did not see suicide as a disgrace. Instead, they classified the methods of suicide according to the types of perpetrators. According to this classification, the hardy rushed to meet death by jumping off cliffs or suffering a blow to the body. Those who did not wish to suffer chose drowning. Those that suffered much in life chose hanging and those with a fiery temperament, perhaps unsurprisingly, would throw themselves into a fire.

❖   ❖   ❖

The oriental Manzi folk were an emotional and sensitive people who were easily affronted by their fellow citizens. If a man were to be insulted by another, even by a minor act, and if the offender happened to be rich and powerful to the extent that the injured party would find it difficult to be vindicated, particular means of retaliation were used. These means however were rather drastic to the injured party as he would seek vindication by hanging himself at the offender's door, this being considered the ultimate insult and expression of contempt. The offender would then be obliged to lay on a lavish funeral, whereby the dead man would get his revenge from beyond the grave as being the cause of so much expense to his enemy.

❖   ❖   ❖

Troglodyte men that were too old to work were expected to commit suicide. They would do this by tying the tail of their ox around their neck and compelling the ox to strangle them. Should any man shirk his responsibility and put off his suicide, a friend, in an act of goodwill, would tie the noose around his friend's neck and attempt to persuade him to take his life. Anyone maimed or diseased held the same responsibility. They too were expected to kill themselves as their society thought it a disgrace to cling to life when unable to accomplish anything worth living for. It was not usual to find anyone above the age of sixty in this tribe of cave dwellers from ancient Ethiopia.

❖   ❖   ❖

A particular Indian tribe inhabiting one of its smaller islands had a law similar to the Troglodytes in which the crippled or infirm were expected to commit suicide. Likewise those reaching the age of one hundred and fifty, an apparently easily achievable age, were also expected to put an end to their life. They had a particularly painless way of achieving this; they would lie down on a particular plant, fall asleep and subsequently die.

❖   ❖   ❖

Mourning:

The Megarians, an ancient city people from Attica in Greece, displayed their grief at losing comrades in battle by shaving off their hair as well as the manes of their horses and mules.

❖   ❖   ❖

The Egyptians went into deep mourning when a pharaoh died. They would cover their heads with dust and mud and fast for seventy days.

❖   ❖   ❖

Professional mourners were hired by the Egyptians to increase the show of respect to the deceased. These mourners, consisting mostly of women, would pretend to cry and show grief.

❖   ❖   ❖

The Egyptians did not permit themselves any luxuries while mourning. This included not taking baths or shaving.

❖   ❖   ❖

Funerals:

Citizens of Tangut, a medieval oriental province, could not be laid to rest after death until the family consulted with an astrologer. The astrologer would take a note of the deceased's date and time of birth and from this information would announce the day on which the corpse must be cremated. Sometimes the family would be lucky and the date would be set soon after death, but they could also be unlucky and told a date of up to six months away. In the latter case the corpse would have to be kept in the family house in a very tightly sealed coffin – tightly sealed in an attempt to prevent the stench of decay. During the time the body remained in the house, the inhabitants would have to continue dishing up food and drink before the coffin at meal times, as if the person were still alive. Finally, when the time came for cremation, the body would be taken to its funeral pyre and burned along with paper images of horses, cattle and coins and any other thing a person might find useful, the idea being that these paper images would accompany the deceased into heaven as tangible objects.

❖ ❖ ❖

When an illustrious Roman citizen died, his funeral cortege would carry him in an upright position to the town forum. Here his son or other close relative would pay tribute to the dead man, listing out all his attributes and virtues, until even the general public would sorely feel the loss of this man. After burial, a life-like mask of the man would be kept in a prominent position in his house. On days of important feasts, these masks would be put out on display, and when another important man died, the masks would be taken to the funeral where they would be worn by men who most closely resembled the original man in both stature and gait. It was intended that the apparent sight of so many past heroes gathered together would inspire the youth.

❖ ❖ ❖

The Prussians, like many other nations, held funeral feasts for their dead. Any food falling onto the ground during one of these feasts was left as a gift for lonely souls who had no relatives to offer them food.

❖ ❖ ❖

Before dispatching their dead, the Troglodytes, a cave dwelling tribe of ancient Ethiopia, would bind together the legs and neck of the corpse with twigs. Then, amid laughter, they would throw stones at the body until it was completely hidden from sight. Finally, they would place a ram's horn on the resultant mound.

❖ ❖ ❖

An Egyptian burial custom dictated that the dead would be judged before being laid to rest in their tomb. This entailed summonsing forty-two judges who would stand before the corpse to adjudicate on the character of the deceased. At this point, it was lawful for anyone to bring an accusation against the deceased. The judges would evaluate the statement and make an assessment. If it was decided that the deceased had led an evil life, he would be deprived of his last rites and resting place. However, if it were found that the accuser had made false claims, he would be severely punished. Following any judgements the mourners would then list out all milestones traversed by the deceased including his education, path in life and various virtues.

❖　　　❖　　　❖

Should an Egyptian lose his life through some accident, the local municipality would be fined the cost of the most extravagant funeral possible. They were considered responsible for the dead body by not having exercised enough care to prevent the accident occurring. The same fines were exerted if the person had drowned or been murdered.

❖　　　❖　　　❖

According to Plutarch, the Egyptians were buried with their innards and other organs having first been removed. The organs were placed in vessels and entombed with the coffin. However the intestines were placed in a separate vessel which, during the funeral rites, had all the iniquities of the person's life heaped onto them (for instance the intestines were blamed for causing glutinous behaviour in the deceased). The intestines would be disposed of separately by being thrown into a river.

❖　　　❖　　　❖

Various ancient writers reported on the procedures followed by the Ethiopians following a death. According to Diodorus of

23

Sicily, the body would be embalmed then coated in a thick layer of glass and stood upright like a pillar for everyone to see. Ctesias of Cnidus disputed this observing that molten glass on a body would burn and disfigure it. Instead, he claimed the body would first be placed in a gold effigy painted to look like the deceased which would then be coated in glass. In a further version of events Herodotus claimed the body was first shrunk, then coated in gypsum, painted to resemble the deceased as closely as possible and then set into a shaft of hollowed out crystal. The corpse was said to be clearly visible through the crystal and free from any kind of smells. The body encased in its crystal coffin would be kept for one year in the house of its nearest relative, then after the prescribed time had elapsed, would be stood up at a spot near the town.

❖   ❖   ❖

After a burial, the medieval Irish would break up the brier used to carry a body to the grave. This was to prevent the fairies coming during the night and taking the body to cavort with them.

❖   ❖   ❖

The body of a king or warrior in ancient Ireland could be buried standing up and fully attired in his arms. The body would be positioned in such a way as to face the territory of its enemy. It was believed that placing the body so would enable the corpse to exercise a malignant effect on the enemy and make them easy to defeat in future battles.

❖   ❖   ❖

Ghosts:
Should crumbs of food fall from an Athenian dining table onto the floor, they would be left where they dropped for any passing ghosts to pick up.

No Prussian would throw rubbish from their front door in case it should hit a passing ghost. A similar belief stopped Greeks from slopping their bath water out their door.

❖   ❖   ❖

The native Alaskan Tlingits would remove corpses from their houses via a specially made hole in the back of their houses. The front door would never be used in case the ghost of the deceased would use it to return to the house.

❖   ❖   ❖

2. Love and Marriage

Kissing:

Egyptians would only slaughter and consume animals that had passed stringent tests for cleanliness. The presence of as much as one black hair on the beast would deem it unacceptable for use. The Greeks however weren't so fussy over what they ate, so as a result an Egyptian would never kiss a Greek for fear of being tainted by the unclean meat they allowed to pass their lips.

❖   ❖   ❖

Dowry:

The concept of a dowry being bestowed upon a bride stretches back centuries and even millennia. In the Ireland of old a very interesting and fair system was set out to ensure that a wife could amass independent means and not have to rely on her husband for money. On their marriage, the new husband would pay a fixed sum to the bride's father. The father would then divide this money evenly between the bride, himself and the head of his clan. Each year the husband would pay this same amount to the father who continued to divide it amongst the family members, but each year giving his daughter a greater share of the total. The payments would continue until the couple had been married for twenty-one years. By this time, the wife would have in her possession enough to support herself comfortably should her husband then decide to trade her in for a younger model! However, if a woman decided to leave her husband at any time for no good reason, then she would have to repay all that the husband had given her over their years of marriage.

❖   ❖   ❖

In the Germany of bygone times, a groom was expected to bring the dowry to a marriage. He was perhaps rather selfish in his choice of gifts for his wife, as the dowry would consist not of pretty trinkets for his bride, but of more practical choices such as oxen and horses, and a little more unusually, weapons and armour! As a man can never have enough of such things, the wife was also expected to bring similar gifts to her husband.

❖   ❖   ❖

Boeotian brides of ancient Greece brought the wheel of a chariot to the bridegroom's house. This was ceremoniously burned as a symbol signifying the permanence of her stay.

❖   ❖   ❖

Marriage:
When it came to marriage the women of Babylon found an ingenious way of ensuring no one would suffer the ignominy of being 'left on the shelf'. Each year all the women of marriageable age would take themselves off to market and put themselves up for auction. When bidding commenced first the most beautiful woman would step forward and offer herself as a lot, ensuring she accepted only the highest bidder as her husband. Offers would run high as it was considered a great mark of esteem for a man to have a pretty wife on his arm. The auction would continue in this manner until all the pretty girls were spoken for – then would come the turn of the more homely women not blessed with such good looks. Now the tables were turned. All the money generated to this point by the beauties of the group would now be used as a dowry for the plainer hopefuls. These would-be brides would auction themselves off to the man prepared to *accept the least* money for her. The thinking was that if a potential husband could not afford a pretty wife, at least he could be compensated for taking an ugly bride!

❖   ❖   ❖

Persian marriages were only consummated at the vernal equinox. On that day, the bride was allowed to eat only a camel's marrow or an apple, but nothing else.

❖   ❖   ❖

The people of Tibet had a very unusual marriage custom. Unlike most other societies the men would not dream of taking a virgin bride. They argued that a woman was worthless unless she had plenty of experience in this area. Furthermore, they thought that a woman who did not have a male admirer willing enough to sleep with her must have displeased the gods in some way. So to give young girls the experience they needed before marrying, mothers would bring their daughters into the camps of foreign travellers and beg the tourists to sleep with the girls. These travellers would choose a selection of girls that took their fancy from amongst this group, leaving the unlucky rejected daughters to miserably return home with their mothers. The girls remaining in the camp would share their favours between any interested man, the deal being that the men would not try to take any of the girls away with them on leaving the area and that having slept with a girl the man would give her some trinket as a memento. These trinkets would be worn by the girl on a necklace, and when she had collected twenty or more she could then look for a husband. The girl with the most tokens, and therefore the most experience, was held in the highest esteem and was prized above all others. This loose behaviour amongst the women stopped as soon as they married, as it was considered highly offensive to touch another man's wife. Marco Polo, who suggested that this country would be a great place for any young lad to visit, documented this unusual custom!

❖   ❖   ❖

Two Tartar men who had the common misfortune of having suffered the loss of a child at an early age, would arrange a marriage between these children, given that one was male and the other female. They would draw up a deed of matrimony between the dead children, then burning it they announced that as the smoke of this deed reached heaven, the children would realise what had been done on their behalf and consider themselves husband and wife. Meanwhile back on earth, the parents would hold a wedding feast, scattering some of the food for the children. They would also offer gifts to the children in the form of horses, clothes and riches which would be drawn on scraps of paper. These drawings would also be burnt, and again as the smoke reached the heavens, the children were believed to receive these gifts. From that point onwards the two families would consider themselves related just as they would have been had their children been alive.

The Spartans were subject to a number of penalties related to marriage. They were punished for not marrying at all, for marrying late in life, or even for having a bad marriage. The latter was defined as being the case when a man married above himself socially so as to secure a rich wife.

❖   ❖   ❖

Tradition amongst western Mediterranean Cantabrarians dictated that women married off their brothers, choosing appropriate wives for them.

❖   ❖   ❖

The formidable Amazons had a marriage law stating that no woman could marry unless she first killed an enemy in battle. The Carmanian men had a similar tradition in that before becoming eligible for marriage, they had first to cut the head off an enemy and bring it to the king. The king would mince the tongue from the head, mix it with a little flour and eat it with the man who had delivered it.

❖   ❖   ❖

The Tapyri men, an ancient Median people, had a custom whereby they would give their wife in marriage to another man once she had borne two or three children to her original husband.

❖   ❖   ❖

Another Median custom dictated that a man could not have less than five wives; likewise it was considered honourable for a woman to have as many husbands as possible. Less than five was considered a calamity.

❖   ❖   ❖

The Greek writer Hesiod believed thirty or over to be a good age for a farmer to marry while he recommended his bride should be nineteen.

❖   ❖   ❖

The happy couple could have chosen any one of three forms of marriage in the early days of the Roman empire. The first involved a ceremony before a priest whereby the couple would make an offering of a spelt cake. The second option involved a fictitious sale in which a father would sell his daughter into service to her husband. The third legal form took place automatically following uninterrupted cohabitation for a full year.

❖   ❖   ❖

The established Roman marriage ceremony started with an animal sacrifice. The entrails of the animal would be 'read' and the results would determine the success or otherwise of the marriage. Without this initial reading, the marriage would be deemed invalid. Following the marriage rites and subsequent celebrations, the bridal party would set out for the groom's home. The groom would throw nuts for the children; these were symbolic of happiness and fertility. Three boys whose parents had to be alive would lead the bride to her destination. Once at the house the bride would be carried across the threshold.

Before her marriage, a Roman bride would part her hair with the blunted head of a spear. The hair was parted because it was considered the favourite haunt of evil spirits and the spear was used as iron was always thought to have magical properties.

❖   ❖   ❖

Wedding gifts given to an ancient Irish couple following their marriage would legally be divided between them. The husband would be entitled to a two-thirds share whereas the bride would receive one-third of the gifts.

❖   ❖   ❖

Affairs:

The people in the oriental province of Kaindu were very welcoming to strangers lodging with them. The extent of their hospitality went as far as encouraging visitors to share their bed with the landlord's wife for the duration of their visit. So as not to cause any embarrassment, as soon as a traveller took lodgings at a house, the husband would take himself off to his fields and there he would remain until the lodger took his leave. The lodger would signal his remaining presence in the house by hanging his cap outside by the door. When the time came for him to leave he would be obligated to make the woman of the house a present of some fine piece of cloth and perhaps a little trinket of some sort. Then as he mounted his horse to ride off, the man and his wife would call mockingly after their departing guest querying exactly what of theirs he took from his visit. While the traveller had nothing but his memories to show for his time as their guest, his hosts were left with, what was to them, a tangible and valuable gift.

❖   ❖   ❖

The ancient Persian tribe of the Massagetae were monogamous as a rule but did also occasionally sleep with the wives of their friends. This was never done in secret however as the man would hang his quiver on the wagon in which he was bedding the woman.

❖ ❖ ❖

The ancient Greeks are known to have regarded male love as more worthy and noble than female love. The men freely conducted love affairs between one another in addition to taking a wife for the sake of producing children. The Cretans followed an unusual procedure in conducting these affairs. If a man was to come across a boy he fancied he would not attempt to gain his affection by persuasion, but would instead abduct the boy. However, the would-be-lover had to inform the boy's friends several days in advance of his intended plan. Nevertheless, despite being armed with this knowledge, it was considered a disgrace for these friends to then try to hide the boy or otherwise thwart his abduction. Instead, when the man came to take the boy, if he was of a socially equal or higher status, the boy's friends would capture the boy and hand him over to his abductor. Should the man be of lower social standing, then the friends would ensure the boy was not captured. If successful, the abductor was required to bestow gifts on the boy before taking him, and anyone else present at the abduction, into the countryside for feasting and hunting. The boy could only be kept for two months after which time he had to be released. On his return to the city, the boy was again plied with gifts, including an ox which was to be sacrificed. At the ensuing feast the boy was able by law to reveal all the details of his sojourn with his abductor and therefore to exact his revenge if he had been treated badly. In this society, it was considered a disgrace for men from established families, or of handsome appearance, not to take a lover.

❖ ❖ ❖

Adultery:
Adultery was very rare in Roman Germany and consequently the punishment was severe when it did occur, particularly for

the women. The husband of an adulterous wife would shave off the offender's hair, strip her naked in front of their relatives and flog her through their village. No matter how young, pretty or rich the woman was, once accused of adultery, she was destined never to find another husband.

❖   ❖   ❖

When husbands from the oriental province of Pem left home on a journey of longer than twenty days duration, their wives were entitled to take another husband in the interim. Likewise, the men were allowed to take another wife on their journey.

❖   ❖   ❖

The nomadic Troglodytes consisted of several cave dwelling tribes in ancient Ethiopia, each ruled by a tyrant. The wives of tribal members were shared, however, anyone committing adultery with the wife of a tribal chief was fined a sheep.

❖   ❖   ❖

The Roman Emperor Augustus attempted to curb the spate of adultery taking place during his reign by passing a law which confiscated half the wealth of both adulterers and forbade them from ever marrying each other. (This pitfall was overcome by divorcing in advance of the anticipated adultery.) The new law was an improvement on that enforced previously which saw the woman's adultery as a crime punishable by death whereas the man was allowed to go unpunished.

❖   ❖   ❖

Divorce:
According to the ancient Irish Brehon law, marriage could be lawfully invalidated by the wife for any one of several reasons. Two of the more unusual reasons were if the husband was obese, as he was not expected to be of much use in the bedroom, and

the other was if the husband was a gossip who would brag of his bedroom antics.

❖ ❖ ❖

Following a divorce an Irish couple would divide their goods according to their original ownership. Any goods attained through an accumulated wealth following the marriage would also be divided. In this case, the wife was entitled to her portion in accordance with her industry during the marriage. So, if she had been a good worker, she was automatically entitled to a ninth share of the goods.

❖ ❖ ❖

If a medieval Irish couple failed to come to an agreement regarding the division of their common goods following a divorce they could bring the case to court. However, the wife was only permitted to sue for items pertaining to a woman. So for instance she was allowed to request the family dog or cat, mirrors, sieves or needles as part of her settlement.

❖ ❖ ❖

'Till Death Us Do Part:

Indian wives were burnt on a pyre with their husband when the husband died. This was intended as a preventative measure to overcome any temptation a wife may have to poison her husband should she find another man.

❖ ❖ ❖

The Trausi people of ancient Thrace followed an unusual custom following a death. When a Trausi man died, his several wives would throw themselves into competition to see which of them was the most grief struck. The man's friends would then judge the wives to determine the one most distraught. The winner received the reward of being slaughtered and buried beside her husband.

34

However the survivors did not get away lightly, they suffered under the disgrace of not having grieved enough for their dead husband.

❖   ❖   ❖

Love-potions:
The brain of a crane was thought to possess a spell-like quality which would lead women to grant sexual favours. Aeolian, the classicist recording this ability, did not specify how the spell ought to be administered!

❖   ❖   ❖

Wives:
The Thracians considered themselves wretched if they did not have a large number of wives – commonly they had ten or eleven wives each. A man unlucky enough to die having only amassed four or five wives was mourned as a poor wretch without a bride.

❖   ❖   ❖

Brothers shared many of their possessions in Felix Arabia. Their property was shared amongst all, but ruled by the eldest. Likewise, they had one wife between them all. The brother arriving home from work first was entitled to sleep with her. He left a sign to his other brothers of his intentions by leaving his staff by the door – custom dictated that all men had to carry a staff in this country. However, the wife would ultimately spend the remainder of the night with the eldest brother.

❖   ❖   ❖

Daughters:
Trausi daughters living in ancient Thrace were allowed to behave just as they pleased when it came to fraternising with the opposite sex. They could sleep around as much as they wished

and with whomever they chose. However, as soon as a woman married she was watched like a hawk by her husband and not allowed any freedoms.

❖   ❖   ❖

Impoverished medieval Taxilians of the Far East with daughters to marry off and who couldn't afford a dowry, would bring their marriageable daughters to the market place where they would attract attention by blowing trumpets and banging on drums. Once a crowd had amassed, the father would begin touting for a son-in-law. Any man stepping forward and expressing an interest would soon get an eyeful as the loving father would raise his daughter's dress and expose her from the shoulders down to her would-be suitor. If the man liked what he saw, and agreed terms with her father, he would then get to marry the girl.

❖   ❖   ❖

Concubines:
The Mongol leader Kublilai Khan was said to have had a fondness for pretty concubines. Every few years he would send emissaries to the north Asian Tartar provinces, extolling them to select for him the most beautiful girls they could find. They would have very strict criteria by which the girls would be chosen which took into account their hair, nose, mouth and so on. Each girl would be graded using a predefined scoring system, with as many as 500 girls assessed in this way. All the girls scoring the highest marks would be summoned to the Great Khans' court. There they would be reassessed and whittled down to thirty or so girls with again those scoring highest going on to their next appraisal. At this stage, they would be doled out singly to the wives of high-ranking court officials who would watch carefully over them for a night to make a final judgement. This last assessment would ensure they had no blemishes, then that they were virgins and finally that they slept without snoring and their breath did not smell! Only those passing this final hurdle would be allowed to associate with the great ruler himself.

3. Staying Healthy

Illness:

A particular tribe of Indians had an unusual if not drastically practical method for dealing with illness and disease. As soon as a member of this tribe showed the first sign of an illness, his nearest and dearest would kill and eat him! This was done to prevent the inflicted person's illness transferring to either their animals or to other tribal members. Women, so often meted out less violent behaviour, weren't exempt from this drastic action either. The not altogether surprising result of this extreme behaviour was that anyone feeling a little under the weather would try their utmost to hide it from their family and friends. And of course, unsurprisingly, there were very few elder members surviving in this particular tribe.

❖　　❖　　❖

It is a fact that there are no snakes in Ireland. But according to an old English belief, anything associated with Ireland had far reaching effects for snakes anywhere. Any person bitten by a snake could cause the poison to subside by steeping the pages of an Irish book in water and then drinking this water.

❖　　❖　　❖

Disease:

Pythagoras advocated living a simple life. He believed that disease came from indigestion which in turn came from extravagance. In fact he believed extravagance ruined both fortunes and health. His advice to his followers was to eat uncooked food and drink only water.

❖　　❖　　❖

The Egyptians believed that disease came from excessive eating and bad diet. For that reason they were careful to maintain a particular diet and exercise which saw them abstaining from certain foods at regular intervals and consuming preventative doses of medicine.

Doctors:

According to Herodotus, there were no doctors in ancient Babylon. In order to affect an appropriate cure when one was required, relatives of the sick would bring them to a roadside where all passers-by were obliged to stop and enquire after the invalid. Any passer-by finding they had suffered an illness with similar symptoms, from which they had subsequently recovered, or even knew of someone else with a similar complaint, was obliged to express an opinion as to how the sick person may be cured.

In a precursor to the modern national health service, the ancient Egyptians worked on a very similar principle whereby the government would pay for the training of doctors, and would continue to pay their salary while they worked. This did not prevent some doctors from trying to earn a little extra by charging some patients. This was tolerated by the authorities to a point. Doctors were not however allowed to charge those in the military or those travelling overseas. In a further similarity to modern practice, doctors specialised in specific areas of health. Women doctors were also common, specialising particularly in areas of 'an internal nature'.

In Ancient Egyptian doctors treated their patients according to a written law; following to the letter directions of old medical journals set out by even more ancient physicians. As long as the doctor remained faithful to these journals, should he have the misfortune of losing a patient, he would be free from any blame. However, if a doctor deviated from the old practices by devising treatments of his own, and then lost his patient, he would be arrested and have to submit to a murder trial. Not surprisingly very few doctors considered themselves wiser than the ancient physicians.

❖ ❖ ❖

Certain oriental provinces of bygone times had no doctors. The people relied instead on magicians to cure them of their ills. These magicians would arrive at a patient's house when summoned, listen to the symptoms, then begin to dance about and leap into the air until eventually one would fall to the ground. It was believed at this point the spirit or devil of the ailment in the patient had entered the prostrate magician. The other magicians would then question the now possessed member of their company, asking what was wrong with the patient. This magician would list all the spirits offended by the patient and would identify which of these were responsible for causing the illness. His fellow magicians would then offer up prayers asking for the restoration of the patient's health. The patient was then either declared beyond help, or encouraged that a cure could be affected. The latter could only occur if the patient's family offered a sacrifice to the spirits during a feast to which the magicians must be invited. In this instance, a great feast would be prepared and the prerequisite number of animals would be sacrificed. At the feast, the magicians would ask again if the patient was to be cured and sometimes they proclaimed that he would, and at other times they would prescribe additional feasts and sacrifices, to which the magicians must of course again be invited.

❖ ❖ ❖

Magicians were used in lieu of doctors in Dagroian, a medieval kingdom of Java Minor. When someone fell ill, the magicians were called in to determine whether this person was destined to live or die. If the patient were diagnosed as being fated to die, his relatives would send for specially appointed men to swiftly dispatch him. This would be achieved by suffocating the unfortunate patient and as if this were not bad enough, the patient would subsequently be cooked. All his relatives would then gather to eat him whole, taking great care to eat everything, even down to the marrow, as they particularly wanted to avoid any part of him remaining which might generate worms. It was considered very unlucky for any part of the dead to produce worms, which they assumed would in turn die once the flesh was consumed. The death of these worms would incur great sin on the man's soul as it could be held to account over their death giving him ultimate responsibility for the souls of the worms.

❖　　　❖　　　❖

A medieval Irish doctor failing to cure a wound through care-lessness, neglect or incompetence had to refund his fee. In addition, he was obliged to pay his patient a sum of money equal in amount to the fine imposed if he had inflicted the wound himself.

❖　　　❖　　　❖

A doctor and his understudy in medieval Ireland could choose to stay in a patient's house during treatment. The patient would be obliged to feed and shelter the medics during their stay as well as pay the fee due for any treatment obtained. However should the treatment be unsuccessful the doctor was obliged to return the fee together with the cost of his maintenance. He would only be exempt from these loses if he had first obtained a guarantee of immunity from the patient.

❖　　　❖　　　❖

Autopsies:

Egyptian doctors were known to have preformed autopsies on their dead to ascertain the causes of death. They also used this examination to learn more about the nature of the human body.

❖   ❖   ❖

Cures:

Inhabitants of the medieval oriental kingdom of Kara-jang believed that the gall taken from the stomach of a crocodile was a powerful cure for many diverse ailments and pains. For instance, it was valued as a cure for the bite of a mad dog and was said to both speed up the arrival of a newborn and to relieve the labour pains of a woman giving birth.

❖   ❖   ❖

The English of the Dark Ages believed that dust settling on the tomb of Chad, if mixed with water, would cure illness.

❖   ❖   ❖

The Nysaeans, an ancient tribe settled in the Far East, had a particular cave near one of their villages that they regarded as sacred. When a Nysaean fell ill he would go to a priest who would sleep on his behalf in this cave. While asleep the priest would dream of the cure needed for the patient to recover.

❖   ❖   ❖

An effective remedy was suggested by the ancient Greeks to anyone bitten by a shrew. Sand taken from a wheel track was sprinkled on the bite and this was thought to provide immediate relief.

❖   ❖   ❖

A Scythian cure for stiff legs involved bleeding the vein behind the ear.

❖   ❖   ❖

To help people recovering from chronic illnesses, the Romans were advised to rock back and forth. This action was thought to be particularly useful for those unable to take exercise. Many sorts of rocking were prescribed depending on the patient's strength and resources! The levels of rocking advised spanned the gentlest, similar to being on board a ship either in harbour or in a river, to the more severe akin to being on board a ship on the high seas.

❖   ❖   ❖

Medieval Irish doctors were subject to fines if their cures were not effective. Certain time intervals had to elapse before the effectiveness of a cure would be judged. These times varied according to the site of the infliction. So for instance an arm wound would be judged after one year whereas an affliction to the head would necessitate three years elapsing. If any relapse to the inflicted area should occur after these times, the doctor would be exempt from responsibility.

❖   ❖   ❖

The ancient Irish had a range of cures for all manner of illnesses. For instance applying a plaster composed of boiled hogs lard, flour, beeswax and egg white mixed with strong ale could cure a sore breast. Brewing a certain mix of herbs, which had been pulled while incanting prayers, with water taken from a spring well, could cure an injury inflicted by a fairy. This concoction had to be drunk in its entirety by the patient while being careful not to spill any of the mix or setting the bowl on the ground before it was finished.

❖   ❖   ❖

Hospitals:

Ancient Irish Brehon law decreed that hospitals had to have four open doors placed so that the patient could be seen from all sides. They had to be free from dirt and have a stream of water flowing through the middle of the floor.

❖   ❖   ❖

While in hospital medieval Irish doctors would decide which particular bed the patient should lie in and what foods must be eaten. The doctor could also insist that the patient be kept away from dogs, fools and female scolds to avoid worry.

❖   ❖   ❖

Wounds:

The ancient Median tribe of the Magi believed that the pain from a wound could be lessened if a nail from a shoe, or indeed anything that had been trodden on, was worn as an amulet around the neck.

❖   ❖   ❖

A Roman household medical book advised cleaning a wound with honey, whereas an application of butter was proposed to heal flesh. Indeed honey has now been scientifically proven to have powerful antiseptic and fungicidal properties and is currently used to promote the healing process.

❖   ❖   ❖

The Romans used a plaster composed of spiders' webs soaked in oil and vinegar to staunch the flow of blood from minor gashes such as those obtained during a trip to the barber.

❖   ❖   ❖

If a person inflicted a wound on another in medieval Ireland, he had to both pay a fine to the injured man and cover medical expenses. The medical treatment could be administered at home or in a hospital, according to the choice of the patient. Should he choose hospital treatment then his mother, if living, was obliged to accompany him. The aggressor would also defray her expenses.

❖ ❖ ❖

Sneezing:

The Romans liked to use vinegar as a remedy for many diverse ailments. The more unusual perhaps extolled the virtues of vinegar as a remedy for sneezing. Apparently inhaling vinegar fumes will stop sneezing. Another interesting fact to note about sneezing is that the Romans also used to respond to a sneeze with the evocation, 'God bless you'. Interesting because the God that was evoked then was very different to the one we now call upon.

❖ ❖ ❖

Indians setting out on a journey would immediately stop in their tracks were they to hear someone sneezing. They would sit themselves down on the roadside waiting to hear a second sneeze, which would counteract the bad omen predicted by the initial sneeze. Should none be forthcoming the traveller would promptly return home and not risk continuing on the journey. The Brahmans, a tribe of India, had the same super-stition, except their counter omen was the sight of a swallow flying above them. With this portent, they would continue the journey, if not, they would return home.

❖ ❖ ❖

Colds:

The Libyans employed an interesting preventative method against the common cold. When their children reached four years of age, the veins on their head were cauterised with a bit of greasy wool. The idea behind this strange action was to stanch the flow of any catarrh that might build up in the head. Should the unfortunate child suffer convulsions because of such a drastic treatment, they would then be treated further by having goat's urine sprinkled over them.

❖ ❖ ❖

Choking:
If a Roman were to find himself choking on a fish bone while eating, his dining companions would attempt to dislodge the bone by thrusting his feet in cold water. Should the bone in question be from another animal, then more bones from the same pot should be applied to the head. It was not specified by Pliny the Elder, who recommended this remedy, if the bones should be applied with force! Even more absurd is the counter for a person choking on a piece of bread. Apparently, to stop choking, pieces from the same loaf ought to be placed into both ears.

❖ ❖ ❖

Dentists:
Dentists practised treatments in ancient Egypt that were not too dissimilar to those found today. Fillings were used to block cavities, and rather extravagantly, gold was the material of choice.

❖ ❖ ❖

Toothache:
Apollonius advocated a rather drastic remedy for relieving sore gums. He suggested scrapping the gums with the tooth of a man who had met a violent death.

❖ ❖ ❖

Eyesight:

The Greeks believed that cabbage was good for their eyesight. The consumption of cabbage was said to improve a person's vision.

❖ ❖ ❖

Eagles have always been renowned for their keen eyesight. This trait was believed to transfer to humans with weak eyesight if the gall of the eagle, mixed with Attic honey, was smeared across the eyes. The recipient was expected to acquire extremely sharp eyesight.

❖ ❖ ❖

Juice extracted from balsam wood was used in Judea to cure headaches and cataracts.

❖ ❖ ❖

A sore eye would be cured in medieval Ireland by extracting the juice from the yarrow and daisy plants and mixing this with the milk taken from a woman who had just given birth to a daughter. The mixture would be left to stand until the evening after it was made, then used to bathe the eye.

❖ ❖ ❖

Poisoning:

According to the Magi, a Median tribe, secretly putting a whetstone (which had previously been used to sharpen iron tools) under the pillow of a man dying from poisoning would cause him to reveal everything about the poisoning but the person responsible. By this method his family could discover what poison had been used, when and where it had been applied, but not who to blame for its administration.

❖ ❖ ❖

Diarrhoea:

The Romans suggested several counters for diarrhoea. One cure extolled rest and the consumption of astringent foods, such as cheese from across the ocean or cabbage boiled twice, followed by a bath, a massage, and then sitting with the shoulder blades towards a fire. Another remedy advised eating and then provoking vomiting to counter the diarrhoea. A more unusual remedy recommended travelling in a carriage or, preferably, riding on horseback to strengthen the intestines.

❖　　❖　　❖

Dysentery:

The ancient Irish believed dysentery could be cured by taking three and a half pounds of iron, making it red hot, then plunging it into three quarts of new milk. This would be left to cool and the procedure repeated three times. Half a pint of the milk remaining would be taken morning and evening.

❖　　❖　　❖

Constipation:

The Romans advocated certain foods as a counter for constipation. These included lettuce, raisins, small fat birds or indeed any fatty meat.

❖　　❖　　❖

Sinews:

To ease tremors of the sinews, Romans were advised to drink water, go for a walk, avoid worry after meals, and be gently massaged. It was stipulated that this gentle massage had to be administered by the hands of boys rather than men.

❖　　❖　　❖

Warts:

According to Pliny, warts can be removed if the inflicted person lies on their back on a path after the twentieth of the month and gaze upwards with their hands stretched back over their head. They must then grab hold of whatever they find in their reach and use this to rub the wart.

❖   ❖   ❖

Epilepsy:
The Roman cure for epilepsy was a lengthy one. They prescribed daily rituals including the avoidance of sunshine, baths, wine, overlooking a cliff, vomiting and anything terrifying. Walking was advised followed by vigorous rubbing with not less than 200 hand strokes. Certain food was to be avoided, however the food consumed by the middle classes was recommended. Rather drastically, it was also suggested that drinking the hot blood from the cut throat of a gladiator would relieve the ailment.

❖   ❖   ❖

Some ancient writers advocated using the discarded skin of a gecko as an effective cure for epilepsy.

❖   ❖   ❖

The medieval English believed their kings had healing powers. In a rite similar to the Maundy Money distributed in modern times, the king would distribute coins on Good Friday. Those receiving the coins would have them made into rings called 'cramp rings', as they believed these had the power to cure muscle spasms and epilepsy.

❖   ❖   ❖

Ulcers:
The Ethiopians thought that stepping into scorpion dung would give them ulcers.

❖   ❖   ❖

The Romans were advised to cure ulcers by eating honey and leeks, going for gentle walks, and avoiding strenuous activities such as running and wrestling.

❖ ❖ ❖

Corns:
If a corn is pared when a star is falling, then the corn is quickly cured

❖ ❖ ❖

Jaundice:
Jaundice could be easily cured with the help of a curlew. To affect a result the jaundiced person was required to stare at a curlew and if his gaze were returned without flinching, he would be cured.

❖ ❖ ❖

Headaches:
Apparently, the Romans believed tying a rope around their head could cure a headache. The rope had to be one used in a hanging.

❖ ❖ ❖

The Romans also believed that pouring vinegar over a door hinge could cure a headache. The vinegar had then to be used to make up a poultice, which they then put on their head.

❖ ❖ ❖

Hygiene:
The Indians of old used each hand for very specific purposes. For instance, they would only use their right hand for eating, never touching food with their left. Only the right hand could come

into contact with something considered clean. Conversely, the left hand was used for all unclean tasks such as wiping their noses, or certain other parts of their anatomy!

❖   ❖   ❖

Warmth:

Keeping a patient warm was the advice for many ailments. The Romans had a surprisingly modern method for doing this. They heated millet, salt or sand which was then poured into a linen cloth bag and given to the patient. Alternatively, 'hot water bottles' were utilised. These were simply leather bags filled with hot oil, or hot water. Earthenware bottles were also used.

❖   ❖   ❖

Madness:

The Romans were advised of several symptoms related to madness in a patient. These signs included speaking hurriedly, breathing slowly and forcefully, frequent movement of the eyes, insomnia and grinding teeth.

❖   ❖   ❖

Spells:

Many peoples would perform counter charms to avoid coming under the influence of magical spells. One such counter involved hard-boiled eggs. On finishing a boiled egg, the empty eggshell would be turned upside-down in the eggcup and the top smashed in. Snail shells were thought to offer similar protection.

❖   ❖   ❖

Pythagoras advocated spitting on nail clippings when discarding them. This action would prevent anyone finding them from utilising the clippings to perform magic against the owner.

❖   ❖   ❖

An unusual belief among many ancient societies involved avoiding leaving visible traces of a person behind. For instance, Pythagoras suggested rolling up the night's bedclothes after rising. This would effectively remove the impression otherwise left by the person on the clothes and thereby remove vulnerability to harm. This policy fell in line with a wider believe that stabbing a person's footprints would render that person lame.

❖   ❖   ❖

Memory:

Followers of Pythagoras trained their memories to improve. The method used involved remaining in bed until the minutiae of their actions on the previous day had been recounted to another. If there were time, they would go back several days and for each relate all activities from dawn to nightfall. In this way, they were adept at recalling even the most trivial fact.

❖   ❖   ❖

4. Looking Good

Washing:

The Asia Minor Scythians had a novel way of conducting their ablutions. When they wanted to clean themselves, they would wash their head with soap but they would cleanse the rest of their body with a so-called vapour bath. This first necessitated setting up a tent like structure by stretching a cloth over a tripod made from three sticks. They would take great care to seal the seams of the cloth as well as possible, then content the structure was reasonably airtight, they would enter the tent with a dish filled with hot stones. Once settled, they would throw hemp seeds onto the stones then sit back and enjoy the smoke given off by the smouldering hemp. Apparently, they enjoyed their bath so much, according to Herodotus, they would 'howl with pleasure'!

❖   ❖   ❖

Should a Roman find his bath to be too hot, he could ward off its effects by holding vinegar in his mouth.

❖   ❖   ❖

The Iberians and neighbouring Cantabrians were said to bathe in urine which had been aged in cisterns. They also used this as a cleanser for their teeth.

❖   ❖   ❖

Hairstyles:

Extreme hairstyles are nothing new. Apparently, some ancient Libyans favoured a style where they would grow the hair on the right side of their head but shave the left.

❖   ❖   ❖

An ancient Greek island people, the Abantes, had a very practical if unusual hairstyle. They cut only the front part of their hair leaving the rest to grow. And the reason – they were a fighting tribe who specialised in hand-to-hand combat. Fighting in such close proximity to their enemy, they found that cutting off the hair growing about their face prevented their opponents from obtaining a convenient and painful handhold on their tresses. Apparently Alexander the Great thought this such a good idea that he ordered his men to shave off their beards for the very same reason.

❖   ❖   ❖

Spartan free men were recognised by the length of their hair as by a legal enactment, only they were permitted to wear it long. Slaves on the other hand wore their hair short.

❖   ❖   ❖

The Egyptians believed their cleanliness could be maintained by keeping themselves well shaved, both their heads and faces. They distinguished themselves from their slaves by insisting their slaves wore long hair and kept beards. They ridiculed anyone not shaving, saying they were slovenly and lazy. Peculiarly however, the Egyptians liked to wear wigs and false beards on occasion.

❖   ❖   ❖

Barbers were an essential element of Roman life, as fashion required all men to be clean-shaven. However securing a good haircut or shave was fraught with difficulties as the tools of the barbers trade were not the most efficient; so much so that a visit to barber could be a bloody operation. In an attempt to invoke greater caution in this trade, the Emperor Augustus legislated for responsibility and damage done following such a visit.

❖   ❖   ❖

So keen were the Romans to appear smooth skinned that they employed other means of depilation to compensate for the ineffectiveness of their razors. Some used tweezers to pluck their beard while others used a depilatory paste which counted ivy gum, ass' fat, bat's blood and powdered viper, amongst its ingredients.

❖   ❖   ❖

The first beard shorn from a young Roman man was ceremoniously deposited in a pyx and a feast was held by family and friends to mark the occasion.

❖   ❖   ❖

On coming of age, Germans would allow their beards and hair to remain uncut. They would only be permitted to shave or cut their hair once they had slain an enemy and thereby displayed evidence of their bravery.

❖   ❖   ❖

A Roman man wishing to dye his hair black may well have chosen to use ravens eggs. However, if this was the method of choice, the accompanying advice was to keep olive oil in the mouth and the lips closed. If this advice was not followed, then the teeth along with the hair would irreversibly turn black.

❖   ❖   ❖

Spartans going into battle ensured their hair was combed and well groomed as they considered it improper to die with untidy hair.

❖   ❖   ❖

An act passed in a medieval Irish court banned the English settlers from wearing moustaches like the 'Irish Enemy'.

Baldness:

Here is an original preventative measure against baldness. The Egyptian male believed they never went bald because of their habit of shaving their head from an early age. They thought that the exposure of their head to the sun thickened their skull which in turn prevented them from going bald.

❖   ❖   ❖

The Romans believed that if they cut their hair on the seventeenth or twenty-ninth of a month this would prevent both hair loss and headaches!

❖   ❖   ❖

A Roman cure for baldness involved cremating a hedgehog and mixing its ashes with pitch. Rubbing this concoction onto the offending area was believed to cause the hair to re-grow.

❖   ❖   ❖

Clothing:

The Egyptian upper classes would not dream of wearing woollen undergarments. Indeed their priests were forbidden from wearing any clothing derived from animal hair on the grounds of cleanliness. Even the dead would never be buried in a woollen garment.

❖   ❖   ❖

It was believed amongst the Romans that a garment made from the wool of a sheep that had been mauled by a wolf would cause the wearer constant irritation.

❖   ❖   ❖

Beauty:

The Indians prized beauty so much that it influenced their choice of monarch. Only the most beautiful man would be chosen by the Indians to be their king.

The Indians applied strict beauty regulations on their offspring. In a precursor to modern bonny baby contests, all Indian babies were judged for their beautiful features at two months old. Those denounced as ugly by the judges, and not as beautiful as the law required, would be promptly put to death.

❖　　❖　　❖

To further beautify themselves, Indians would dye their beards with the most florid colours they could find.

❖　　❖　　❖

Vain Romans would visit their barbers in an attempt to improve their looks. The barbers did not only shave and dress the hair of their customers, they also disguised flaws. A man whose skin was not as attractive as he wished would have little patches of cloth glued over the offending blemish.

❖　　❖　　❖

Birthmarks:
Medieval Europeans believed that both kings' and sorcerers' sons bore a red birthmark on their right shoulders which distinguished them from other men.

❖　　❖　　❖

Tattoos:
Tattoos were considered very desirable and the mark of breeding by the Trausi people inhabiting ancient Thrace. Only the rich and socially elevated were tattooed whereas those born to more humble means were left tattooless.

❖　　❖　　❖

The eastern Kaugigu people also regarded tattooing as a sign of breeding. The greater the number of tattoos, the more handsome the person was considered. Tattooing necessitated the recipient to be bound hand and foot and held down as the tattooist set to work. The designs would first be sketched on the person's body, then the tattooist would tie several needles together, then prick out the pattern. The procedure was not without its downside: many of the subjects subsequently died through loss of blood.

❖   ❖   ❖

The Call of Nature:
Egyptians, contrary to many other societies of the time, would eat outdoors and relieve themselves indoors. The reasoning behind this behaviour was that they thought any action they considered unseemly ought to be done in private, out of sight of the general public.

❖   ❖   ❖

The medieval Irish referred to the room containing the toilet as the veil house. A certain order of monks believed that this room was the home of demons. In order to protect themselves they were required to both bless the demons and themselves each time they needed to make use of the privy.

❖   ❖   ❖

Mirrors:
Pliny believed that the phenomenon of mirrors, that is their ability to reflect a likeness, was due to air bouncing from the surface of the mirror and making contact with the eyes.

❖   ❖   ❖

Diets:
The young men of ancient Celtica were given a good incentive for watching their figures. They were required by law to maintain a certain physique and would be punished should they become fat or potbellied and exceed the standard waist measurement dictated by the government.

5. Food and Drink

Cooking:
The Scythian landscape proved somewhat problematic when meat was on the menu as there was a lack of firewood in their barren environment of north-western Asia Minor. As a result, they had to devise alternative methods for lighting fires to cook their meat. And the solution – they got their meat to cook itself. First, they would skin the animal then de-bone it. The resulting fillets would be put into a cauldron and the bones put underneath and set alight. If no cook pot was to be found, no problem, the meat would simply be put back into the skin together with some water and the whole bladder boiled over the bones. In this way, the animal could be contrived to cook itself!

❖   ❖   ❖

It was believed in ancient times that kissing a red mullet before cooking it would ensure its stomach would not burst when it was being cooked.

❖   ❖   ❖

Spices:
Cinnamon was a spice always in demand. It was favoured by the ancient civilisations as much as it is today. According to Herodotus, the Arabians were responsible for collecting and selling the spice, although their means of gathering the cinnamon was undoubtedly unique. It was reported that the cinnamon sticks were gathered by large birds which used them to build their nests. As the nests were built on mountain faces it was impossible for anyone to climb up to retrieve the cinnamon sticks, so the industrious Arabians would cut up large joints of meat and leave them below the nests. When spotted, these birds – especially the phoenix – would swoop down, collect the

meat and bring it back to their nests. The weigh of the meat would then bring down the nests and the Arabians waiting below would rush in and gather the cinnamon scattered about the ground. Pliny the Elder however was a little more cynical. On recounting this story, he suggested that this notion was proliferated to exaggerate the rareness of the spice and so artificially inflate its price.

❖   ❖   ❖

Eating Out:
Spartan men considered eating out most beneficial as it meant they would not be able to over indulge with alcohol. They had a very pragmatic reason for believing this. They reasoned that eating out necessitated a walk home at the end of the evening as of course they could not sleep where they were. Bearing this fact in mind, they knew that to get home safely through the dark streets they would have to watch how much they drank and remain relatively sober.

❖   ❖   ❖

Table Manners:
Roman philosophers believed it was wise to give in to nature and belch if needed while at the table. A particular Roman emperor carried this a step further and decreed that all emissions of wind were authorised as acceptable. The doctors of the day advised that people should take advantage of this edict while it lasted.

❖   ❖   ❖

The Irish upper classes always took great care in seating their family and guests to dinner. They had to be placed strictly according to rank as any deviation or perceived snub could lead to quarrels or even war.

❖   ❖   ❖

Alcohol:

Pliny reported with amazement that the western peoples had concocted a brew from grain soaked in water when grapes were not available to them for making wine. He marvelled at the wonderful ingenuity man possesses that he has even discovered how to make water intoxicating! Tacitus also commented on this ability to convert water and grain into alcohol, but remarked that the Germans showed no self-control when drinking.

❖   ❖   ❖

Roman woman were prohibited from drinking wine. In order to catch them out if suspected of drinking, their male relatives would kiss the women to see if they could detect any wine on their breath.

❖   ❖   ❖

Roman citizens were given strange advice regarding the storage and use of their wine. Apparently, jars of wine ought not be opened in mid winter except if the day was fine with a south wind blowing. Otherwise, they were advised to wait until there was a full moon.

❖   ❖   ❖

Aristotle observed that those who were drunk from wine keeled over onto their faces while those under the influence of beer lay on their backs.

❖   ❖   ❖

It was considered fatally unlucky to leave a ladle in a mixing bowl when drinking.

❖   ❖   ❖

Athenus observed that the Egyptians used to eat cabbage to stimulate their palette before drinking.

The Persians would only discuss their most important topics when drinking wine. They considered decisions made whilst under the influence as being more worthwhile and lasting than decisions made when they were completely sober.

❖   ❖   ❖

Hangover Cure:
A Roman medical book advised abstinence from food and drink as a hangover cure. It also extolled the consumption of plenty of water. If a headache persisted then provocation of sneezing was suggested. Should a headache persist to a second day, then more drastic action was advised. The patient was told to shave his head and have water continuously poured over it, and if further relief were needed the temples should be plucked at and the legs rubbed. The head should also be rubbed smartly no more than fifty times. Once the remedy worked, the patient could return to wine, but only having first drunk some water.

❖   ❖   ❖

Onions:
The Athenian statesman Callias recommended the eating of onions just before going into battle advocating their ability to inspire courage.

❖   ❖   ❖

The distinguished Spartan Charmidas considered onions to be a useful method of tricking a jealous wife into believing her husband remained loyal while he was away from home. If he came home with his breath smelling of onions, his wife would believe that it was unlikely he could have got close enough to a woman to get up to anything she should worry about.

❖   ❖   ❖

Meat:
The people of Fu-chau, a medieval eastern coastal province, ate meat of all descriptions, including human flesh. However, they

61

were fussy about their cannibalism, drawing the line at eating the flesh of a person who had died a natural death. What they did consider a great delicacy however, was eating the corpse of a person who had died from a fatal a wound.

❖   ❖   ❖

Bread:
The Egyptians used to knead both bread and a paste they used as a type of pasta with their feet. They found they could make a more liquid dough this way as opposed to hand kneading. Conversely, they mixed the mud used by them for buildings with their hands.

❖   ❖   ❖

Beans:
Beans were never sown and certainly never cooked, even if growing wild, by the ancient Egyptians. Their aversion to this pulse, an aversion shared by Pythagoras, was due to its tendency to cause flatulence.

❖   ❖   ❖

Rice:
To protect their rice crops the Indians took an oath saying that they would never remove rice from the threshing floor before it had been roasted. In this way, the exportation of seed was prevented.

❖   ❖   ❖

Crops:
Certain tribes in India cultivated crops together. Following the harvest they would collect what they had grown and bring it to a common location from which each family would take home whatever they needed to subsist for a year. Anything left over would then be burned so that they would have work to do the following year and not be tempted into idleness.

Oxen are inclined to eat the corn they thresh. In order to stop them consuming their crops, ancient farmers were advised to smear dung over the noses of the oxen. It was hoped that they would be so disgusted by the smell, it would curb their appetite.

❖   ❖   ❖

Famine:
When the Lydians, a people of Asia Minor, were going through a period of famine they devised a means by which they could take their minds off their hunger. They would invent games that they would diligently play every second day, the day on which they did not eat.

❖   ❖   ❖

6. Society

Class:

Any Egyptian dallying or meddling in an occupation, other than the one in which they had been brought up, was severely punished as they believed this deviation would encourage avarice. Conversely, adherence to a predestined occupation ensured the worker would grow to excel in his given trade.

❖　　　❖　　　❖

The swineherds of ancient Egypt were considered to be on the absolute lowest rung of society. No one of a different sphere would marry their daughter to a swineherd and he was considered so impure he was not even permitted entrance into a temple.

❖　　　❖　　　❖

Persians would greet each other in a manner dictated by their rank and place in society. They would kiss those of equal rank when meeting on the street. A cheek would be proffered for a kiss if the acquaintance was of a lower rank, while those of the lowest rank merely received a bow.

❖　　　❖　　　❖

The ancient Irish submitted to exact regulations regarding the colour of their clothing. This was dictated according to their class or rank in society. A slave could only dress in one colour, a peasant in two colours and so forth up to the monarchs who were permitted to wear six colours.

❖　　　❖　　　❖

Respect:

The Greeks had a law requiring all young men to give up their seat or step out of the path of their elders as a mark of respect.

❖ ❖ ❖

The people of Cathay demanded such a high level of respect by children towards their parents that a specific department of state existed solely to punish those upsetting their parents in any way.

❖ ❖ ❖

Male children of ancient Britain were not permitted to approach their father in public until they were of age for military service. It was considered unbecoming for a boy to publicly stand in his father's presence.

❖ ❖ ❖

As a mark of respect the ancient Irish would stand when a person entered the room. However, if they wished to show some, but not total, respect they would merely raise a knee.

❖ ❖ ❖

The Irish of olden times had a variety of ways in which they manifested respect for another. On meeting someone, giving three kisses on the cheek was a sign of affectionate salutation. However, to also place the head on another's chest was to show greater respect and affection.

❖ ❖ ❖

The greatest respect an Irishman could show to another was manifest by carrying that person for some distance by piggyback.

❖ ❖ ❖

Disrespect:
The Egyptians would show their contempt to anyone with whom they experienced dissatisfaction by drawing a picture of this person on the sole of their shoe. In this way, they could walk about all day treading on their enemy.

❖   ❖   ❖

Religion:
The Greeks prayed to gods of the heavens and of the underworld. When praying they would stand with their arms outstretched above them, but their hands would be turned in the direction of the god they evoked. Thus if praying to the gods residing in the heavens, their palms would face upwards whereas if their prayers were directed to the underworld, their palms would face downwards.

❖   ❖   ❖

Priests:
Clergy of medieval England not wishing to remain in the priesthood had all signs of their sanctity removed. This included a new hairstyle to obscure their tonsure, and more drastically, the skin from the tips of their fingers was shaved off as this skin had been in contact with the holy oil when the priest had originally been ordained.

❖   ❖   ❖

The faithful of medieval Greenland had to improvise their religious rites due to shortages of both ordained clergy and mass offertory gifts. To overcome a scarcity of wine for transubstantiation during mass, the pope of the day decreed that beer could be substituted. The shortage of priests posed further problems, as certain sacraments could not be performed in their absence. So for instance, when a Greenlander died with no priest present he could not receive the last rites. Instead, the corpse would be buried without ceremony, but with a pole set vertically through the earth with its end alongside the body. The top of the pole protruding from the ground would effectively mark the grave so that when a priest would eventually be in the vicinity he would simply pull up the pole and pour holy water down the hole onto the body while administering the last rites.

❖ ❖ ❖

English priests have not always enjoyed a good reputation with respect to their behaviour. While sobriety amongst the priesthood was extolled as a virtue, it was not always adhered to, so as a compromise priests were advised at least not to say mass while under the influence.

❖ ❖ ❖

Europeans held several superstitions against the clergy. For instance, priests were associated with death so anyone passing a clergyman would immediately cross themselves to counter the bad luck. It was also considered bad luck to pass a priest on the right side, while in Denmark priests were thought responsible for bad weather and infections.

❖ ❖ ❖

Druids:
The druids of ancient Britain were exempted from military service and from paying taxes. Because of these privileges, many parents sent their children to follow in this profession.

❖ ❖ ❖

Tribes:
The historian Strabo documented some very unusual tribes reportedly living in the area around the Ganges. Apparently, one particular tribe supposedly consisted of members who possessed no mouths. They did however have noses which they used to get their sustenance since they survived by breathing

the vapours of roasting meat and the perfume of fruit. The downside – apparently they felt pain when breathing in bad odours! This imaginative historian also documented a tribe with ears so big they extended all the way to their feet. But there was one apparently useful facet in having such big ears, they were used for sleeping in at night. It was not specified if they were used as hammocks or blankets!

❖   ❖   ❖

The ancient Chelonophagi people of the Persian Gulf lived under turtle shells so large they could also be used as boats. Some members of this tribe also made homes out of the great quantity of seaweed that was washed onto their shores. They had such an affinity with the sea that when a kinsman died, he would be thrown out to sea as food for the fish.

❖   ❖   ❖

Relatives:
It was unwise to fall out with relatives in the ancient northern kingdom of Scythia. A quarrel could lead to a kinsman being swiftly dispatched. This would be followed by a ritual whereby the dispatcher would slice the skull from a point just under the eyebrows, skin it, scoop out the brains and use it thereafter as a cup. These skull cups would be brought out when visitors came by, prompting the owner to detail their bravery in acquiring such an item.

❖   ❖   ❖

Idleness:
The most revered members of the ancient Thracian Trausi society were those who were bone idle. The more work a man did, the less he was respected. In their estimation a worker, such as an agricultural labourer, was a person least worthy of attention.

Education:

The ancient Indian tribe of Brachmanes had an interesting approach to educating their young. A learned man would visit a pregnant woman and conduct lessons with the child while it was still in the womb. After it was born, the child would then continue its lessons with a second tutor until it learned all it could, it would then be passed onto more and more accomplished teachers as it grew older.

❖   ❖   ❖

Apparently there were no scientists in the India of bygone times, as the natives would not study any of the sciences but medicine. The reason, they considered too much training in this field as wicked.

❖   ❖   ❖

It is widely known that the Spartans led a pretty austere life. Spartan means of educating their boys in methods of war were also harsh. Boys would not be fed, instead they had to steal food to survive. It was thought that this would give them the skills they needed in conflict such as stealth, resourcefulness and daring. As an added advantage, Spartans also believed that a starvation diet helped develop the physique. A lean physique was associated with the freeness in which a body could breath. It was thought that over-eating produced a laboured breath and therefore a broad squat frame. Contrarily, if breath could pass freely into the body, it would result in a tall and lean body.

❖   ❖   ❖

The ancient Greeks began the education of their young with poetry, as they believed it would impart moral discipline. The reason being, they considered their poets to be the wisest of men.

❖   ❖   ❖

Phoenicians would not give bread to their children unless they could first hit it using a sling-shot. Thus, they trained their children in the proficient use of weapons at a young age.

❖   ❖   ❖

Schoolmasters of ancient Ireland would foster their pupils for a fee. The master was then obliged to teach his charges all he knew as well as feed and clothe them. A pupil in return was obliged to pay his master all money earned while under his tutelage as well as give him his first fee earned having left school.

❖   ❖   ❖

Having fostered pupils, Irish schoolmasters retained a claim on their students. These educationally based foster children had to support their former masters in old age if poverty rendered it necessary.

❖   ❖   ❖

Wisdom:
The sages of Persis, an ancient country in south-western Persia, believed that a man exhibiting the virtue of self-control would receive an abundance of blessings.

❖   ❖   ❖

The Indian Brachmane philosophers would talk to anyone willing to listen to their wise words. However, when listening to a philosopher the listeners were forbidden to talk, cough or spit. If they did, they would be then prohibited from associating with the philosopher for the rest of that day.

❖   ❖   ❖

Regret:
The Romans believed that if they struck a person and then

immediately regretted their actions, spitting into the hand that inflicted the blow would lessen the resentment of the person struck.

❖   ❖   ❖

Army:
Spartan soldiers were not allowed to keep their shields with them when they were on guard duty as it was thought that exposing the soldier in this way would ensure they remained alert and less prone to falling asleep on duty.

❖   ❖   ❖

Before going into battle, the Macedonians would purify their army by marching them between the severed portions of a dog.

❖   ❖   ❖

Wars:
The unlucky prisoners of war of ancient Athens would have their right thumbs cut off to prevent them from ever being able to hold a spear again. However, this infliction was designed so as not to prevent them from holding an oar when they were set to work on the galleys. Interestingly the Aborigines meted out the same punishment to their enemies. They would also cut the right thumb off an enemy to prevent him from brandishing a spear.

❖   ❖   ❖

A Scythian soldier would drink the blood of the first person he killed. Following a battle, defeated enemies would be decapitated and their heads taken to the king who would share out the loot acquired from the battle according to the number of heads possessed by each soldier. Then, mirroring the approach taken on dispatching a relative, the skull of the worst enemies would be sliced in such a manner as to allow the top of the skull to be fashioned into a drinking cup.

❖   ❖   ❖

Invasion:
When the Persians invaded and captured an island or city, they would 'net' the inhabitants. This was affected by the soldiers who would hold hands, form a line, and advancing systematically across the territory.

❖   ❖   ❖

Fights:
Should the Troglodytes, a cave dwelling tribe of ancient Ethiopia, find themselves fighting between themselves the old women of the tribe would intervene and stand between the combatants. This would ensure that the fight broke up immediately as it was illegal to strike a woman.

❖   ❖   ❖

Courage:
The Scythians, an ancient people who lived in Asia Minor, placed a high value on courage. Once a year the governor of an area would gather the men folk together. He would mix a large bowl of wine and all those who had killed an enemy in battle would be permitted to take a drink. Those who had killed no one were made to sit in disgrace and not allowed any wine. On the other hand, those who had courageously killed a great many enemies were held in high regard and allowed two cups of wine which he would drink simultaneously.

❖   ❖   ❖

Luck:
Apparently, the Romans considered it lucky for a man to spit on his urine while relieving himself. It was also considered

lucky to spit in a right shoe before putting it on and finally, when passing a place where danger had been confronted in the past.

❖   ❖   ❖

The Romans considered it lucky to cut their nails on Rome's market day, but only if they cut in silence, starting with the first digit.

❖   ❖   ❖

Any barons entering the court of Kublilai Khan, the great Mongol leader, were very careful not to stand on the threshold as they walked into his great hall as to do so was considered a very bad omen. Two guards were appointed to stand at the doorway to watch that guests stepped into the hall carefully and no one inadvertently touched the threshold of the door. Should someone even accidentally brush against the threshold, the guards would either confiscate their clothing, relinquishing these only on payment of a fine, or dispense a predefined number of blows on the perpetrator. Conveniently however, as most guests tended to leave the hall in a drunken state, and so could not be expected to control their feet, the superstition was not enforced on the way out.

❖   ❖   ❖

Well-to-do visitors of fine stature lodging with natives of Kara-jang, an old province of northern Cathay, would have to be wary of their hosts when sleeping, as many would not be alive in the morning. Not that the Kara-jangians would be interested in robbing their lodgers, what they sought was the visitor's 'good shadow'. The believe was that intelligence, grace, soul and other good attributes possessed by the visitor would be left in the house with his 'good shadow' should he die there.

❖   ❖   ❖

The people of Ely, a Kingdom in India, had an interesting reception awaiting any ship docking unexpectedly at one of their harbours; the ship would be boarded and robbed of all its cargo. The inhabitants of Ely offered a strange explanation for their behaviour, they considered that fortune had diverted the ship from its course and driven it onto their shores. By this token, they felt justified in making the most of their good fortune and taking possession of the cargo.

❖   ❖   ❖

Pliny advised the Romans to take a bean with them to an auction, as this would bring luck.

❖   ❖   ❖

An owl following a man setting out on business was considered bad luck in ancient Rome.

❖   ❖   ❖

Astrology:

The Egyptian Ptolemy chronicled the effect various planets and astrological signs had on the countries they were thought to dominate. Their influence was believed to be felt by the inhabitant of these countries making them prone to certain national characteristics. So, according to Ptolemy, Britain, Gaul and Germany were influenced by the planet Mars and had an affinity with the astrological sign of Aries. This was thought to make these nations fierce, headstrong and bestial. The Italians were thought to be ruled by the sun and Leo, making them masterful, benevolent and co-operative. The Spanish were associated with Jupiter and Sagittarius, causing them to be independent, simplistic and clean. Cyprus was affiliated to Venus and Taurus, making them luxurious, clean and attentive to the body. The Greeks were ruled by Virgo and Mercury, making them better at reasoning and fond of learning. The Macedonians, connected to Saturn and Capricorn, were

74

therefore acquisitive and mild mannered or very social. Persians and Babylonians were inclined to be concupiscent, ardent and effeminate in dress and adornment. The Indians and Arians were predisposed to be unclean, ugly and bestial while natives of Syria, Judea and Felix Arabia were prone to be gifted in trade, unscrupulous, treacherous, fickle and cowardly.

❖   ❖   ❖

The position of planets was thought to influence human behaviour. This was especially the case when the planets were out of their usual alignment. When this occurred, the planets were supposed to cause diseases of the soul. More specifically, when Mars or the sun deviated from their normal positions it was thought to cause madness. Jupiter and Mercury out of alignment were responsible for causing epileptic fits in those prone to such attacks. Venus induced divine possession and public confessions while Saturn and the moon gave rise to demonic possession and rather peculiarly, water gathering. More generally, other traits could be seen which included the alienation of friends, renting of clothing and the use of abusive language.

❖   ❖   ❖

Wealth:
The inhabitants of Albania were said to be unusually large and handsome and not at all mercenary. In fact, not only did they not use coined money, they could not even count above one hundred.

❖   ❖   ❖

The Egyptians had a simple test which they used to determine whether or not a particular item was made of gold. They would rub the object in question on a piece of basalt; if it left no mark on the stone then it was gold.

❖   ❖   ❖

Law forbade the women of ancient Rome to have any involvement in banking matters.

❖ ❖ ❖

Poverty:

The Tartars of northern Asia were very abrupt towards the poor in their society. They would brush them aside with curses on any encounter, claiming that if God loved the poor man as he did the rich, he would have blessed them with prosperity also. For this reason the better off Tartars never gave money to the poor.

❖ ❖ ❖

Debt:

No Egyptian soldier could be imprisoned for debt. This law was derived to safeguard heads of defence from the possibility of arrest by civil powers.

❖ ❖ ❖

The Egyptians placed little regard on usurers and tried to discourage the practice of accumulating debt. To this end a law was passed making it illegal to borrow money without first making over the body of the debtor's father, as well as the family tomb, as collateral. This gave an added incentive to swiftly repay the money borrowed as it was considered disgraceful to disrespect parents in any way. As an additional incentive, the law also dictated that while the money was outstanding no other family member could be interred if they should die, as technically the family tomb was not in their possession.

❖ ❖ ❖

The medieval Irish had periods during which they were exempt from paying a debt. All debtors were for instance exempt while they attended a fair. Other periods of exemption included set times following the death of a king or chief. So for instance after the high king of Ireland or archbishop of Armagh died there was a period of one year's respite from paying a debt.

A provincial king's death gave an exemption period of three months whereas a local king or chief gave one month. These kings and chiefs could also benefit from these periods of exemptions during their lifetime. At any time they could invoke their right to a period of exemption that would be equal to the period given to their subjects after death.

❖   ❖   ❖

Provision was given to the family of an Irish man dying with a large debt. This provision, termed the Rights of the Corpse, was designed to protect the family from becoming totally destitute. Under this prerogative, the corpse had a right to a cow, a horse, a garment and furniture. These goods belonged outright to the body and could not be taken in settlement of a debt. They could however be passed to the next of kin.

❖   ❖   ❖

Communication:
Communication within the Atlas tribe of ancient Africa must have been particularly difficult. Apparently, the tribesmen had no individual names, and what's more they reportedly had no voice and just made a shrill noise when they spoke.

❖   ❖   ❖

The peoples in the orient of the Middle Ages had a very efficient postal system. Their provinces were criss-crossed with numerous postal stages, allowing messages to travel across the country at quite high speeds. Riders on horseback linked many of these staging posts, but runners connected some also. In these cases, a clever method was devised to ensure the mail travelled to its destination without delay. Staging posts, which were set three miles apart, would dispatch a courier with a letter. The courier would wear a large belt around his waist upon which were fastened a number of bells. As he ran these bells would jangle and when he came close to the next stage, the courier there would hear the bells and ready himself so ensuring that the moment the first man arrived, the next would take the letter and run his leg of the journey. And so the relay would continue, passing the letter from its source to its destination without delay.

❖　　❖　　❖

Commerce:

When a Zar-dandan had dealings with a tradesman these medieval eastern people would strike a deal on the goods or services offered and mark the transaction on a piece of wood. This stick would then be split with both parties taking half each. When time came for settling the payment, the customer would demand back the other half of the stick in return for the money owed.

❖　　❖　　❖

The fullers of Rome were tradesmen who ran laundry services. The central requirement essential to plying this service was a steady supply of urine which was used to soak the laundry. In order to assure a good stock, the fuller bought permission from the authorities to leave cut down jars outside the shop for passers-by to use at their convenience. Many individuals were happy to thus supply the fullers as the alternative necessitated paying to use a public latrine.

❖　　❖　　❖

Modesty:

The young women of Cathay were very modest to the extent that they went out with their eyes downcast and their faces hidden by hoods.

The maidens of Cathay were very keen to preserve all physical signs of their virginity to the extent that when they walked they ensured that they never extended one foot further than a finger's width from the last.

❖ ❖ ❖

The ancient Libyan tribe of the Machlyes held an annual festival where their girls would divide themselves into two teams and fight each other with sticks and stones. Should any girl come to harm, or if the fight resulted in a fatality, it was considered proof that the girl hurt was not a virgin.

❖ ❖ ❖

Services:

The Kinsai, dwellers of a city in the medieval oriental province of Manzi, had an effective fire service. Guards, always on the look-out, were stationed in posts all around their city. At each guard post, there was a large drum and at the first sign of a fire, or indeed any other problem, the guards would beat on the drum thus summoning help. So fearful were the inhabitants of Kinsai of fire breaking out in their city that a curfew was set on the times when domestic fires were allowed to be lit. Patrols of guards would walk the streets watching for signs of fires being burnt passed the allotted time. Should they spot a household flouting the rules they would put a mark on the door of the house. Then next morning the householder would be summons in front of the magistrate to explain himself.

❖ ❖ ❖

Ships:

Ships travelling between China and India were made differently from western ships with unusual methods of caulking the vessels. Rather than using the normally common pitch, a mixture of hemp and lime was pounded together with tree oil which acted as a binder. Each year, maintenance would be carried out on the vessel. A layer of planks would be nailed on top of the existing structure and the whole ship re-caulked. After six years, by which time six new skins would have been added to the ship, the vessel was scrapped as it was not then considered seaworthy.

❖   ❖   ❖

Before setting sail for India, the Chinese would perform a certain ritual to discover if the voyage would prove lucky. A wicker frame would be constructed, then fastened to a long length of rope. Then as a storm whipped up a drunk would be found and lashed to this frame. The frame would be stood upright before the wind which would catch it like a kite bringing both frame and man up into the air. Several men on the ground would hold onto the connecting rope, letting it out bit by bit. If the wickerwork climbed straight upwards for the whole length of the rope, it was considered a good omen – the voyage would be successful. Merchants seeing this would queue up to book space on this ship. However if the frame refused to rise then it was considered unlucky, the ship would be expected to be beset by disasters, and no trader would use the ship forcing it to remain in port that year.

❖   ❖   ❖

Homes:
The front doors of ancient Greek houses opened outwards – onto the street. Consequently when they wanted to leave their homes they had to knock on their door to warn any passers-by that the door was about to be swung open. Contrarily, Roman doors had to open inward. They could only install an outwardly opening door with special permission.

❖   ❖   ❖

Census:

The inhabitants of Cathay established a clever method of moni-toring both the population and the movements of individuals around the country. Each household was obliged to keep a list nailed to the door of their house detailing all occupants together with a tally of the number of horses owned. As babies were born, they would be added to the list and as family members died, they would be struck from the list. In this way, the local rulers would have the means of remaining informed of the population. Those running boarding houses or inns were also obliged to keep lists. They would note down the names of travellers staying with them together with the dates they stayed. In this way, the movements of strangers or travellers could be tracked across the country.

❖　　❖　　❖

Coming of Age:

When an Indian boy reached the age of thirteen he was turned out of the house by his father who claimed that the boy was old enough to earn his living. The boy could go on sleeping in the family home, but he was not to be fed at his father's expense. These boys would tout for work, acting as runners or go-betweens in trade. With the money earned, the boy would buy himself food which he would take home for his mother to prepare and cook for him.

❖　　❖　　❖

Cities:

The king of Thrace founded a city, the name of which translates as 'City of Villains', which he populated with about 2,000 men who were, according to Theopompus, false witnesses, false accusers, lawyers and all other bad men.

❖　　❖　　❖

Traffic was as much of a problem in ancient Rome as it is today. The narrow roads, through which all progress had to be made, whether on foot or when transporting goods, exasperated the problem. To combat these problems Caesar decreed that within a period stretching from sunrise to dusk, no cart was allowed in the inner city. The only traffic allowed during this time was pedestrians or people on horseback. This did alleviate the city's traffic problem but also contributed to a general insomnia experienced each night by citizens lying in bed listening to the commotion of tradesmen's carts trundling along the cobbled streets.

❖   ❖   ❖

Entertaining:

Rich Egyptians had an interesting if not bizarre treat lined up for their guests during the course of a sumptuous dinner party. These imaginative hosts would supply their parties with great quantities of top quality food and drink, and as their guests tucked in, the hosts would reveal a lifelike effigy of a corpse in a coffin. They would take pains to remind their guests that this was how they too would look when they were dead and would remind them of the transient nature of pleasures! The more lavish the party the larger and more realistic the effigy.

❖   ❖   ❖

At some Egyptian banquets the mummy of a dead relative would be propped up at the dinner table as a guest. They had no qualms over confronting their mortality in this way.

❖   ❖   ❖

It was considered very unlucky to mention fire at a Roman banquet. In order to counter any potential misfortune water would be immediately poured under the table if any transgressions were made.

It was considered unlucky to sweep the floor when a Roman guest was leaving a banquet, or to remove a table while a guest was still drinking.

❖   ❖   ❖

Guests at a Roman banquet would fall silent if the number of those present became even. An even number of guests at a banquet was said to spell danger to the reputation of all those present.

❖   ❖   ❖

Both the Greeks and Egyptians considered it bad manners to sit down immediately to a meal on arriving at a house to which they had been invited for dinner. Instead, before indulging they took care to praise and admire all the contents of the room that had been specifically left out for them to admire!

❖   ❖   ❖

Roman emperors each tried to outdo each other with the amount of public entertainment they provided for their people. Certain feast days were observed from antiquity, but these were steadily added to with each successive ruler. At one stage a point was reached whereby one hundred and fifty-nine days were marked out as public holidays. The majority of these games were provided for the public's entertainment and paid for from the treasury.

❖   ❖   ❖

Romans believed an argument could be started at a dinner party if someone dropped a stone which had been bitten by a dog into the wine jar. This would cause a fury to break out between the dinner guests.

❖   ❖   ❖

In the royal halls of the ancient Irish both men and woman would eat in the same room, but seated at different tables. However, it was common on these occasions for the women to wear masks to partially hide their face.

❖   ❖   ❖

Music:
Egyptians considered music to be useless and even worse – harmful to boys! This was because they believed listening to music made the spirit of the listener effeminate.

❖   ❖   ❖

In parts of Egypt, the trumpet was never used as a musical instrument because it was thought to sound like a braying ass.

❖   ❖   ❖

Dance:
Upper-class Egyptians did not participate in any form of dancing, believing it to be uncouth. They left this form of expression to the lower classes. In fact, they were not alone in this belief, as Roman dignitaries also believed dancing ought be left to the lower ranks of society, drunks, or the insane! However, the Greeks had a fondness for dance, as long as the movements did not make them look effeminate.

❖   ❖   ❖

Actors:
During a certain era in the history of ancient Rome actors were so popular that riots would break out in their name. At one point, in an attempt to quell their influence, the authorities banned them from the city.

❖   ❖   ❖

The Roman public had an appetite for realistic, particularly violent, drama. So, when a sword fight was to be played out on stage the actors used real weapons and pulled no punches. When a tragedy was depicted where the protagonists met a bloody end, the actors would play out the scene to a point, then one of their number would be substituted for a convicted criminal who would be executed on stage in front of the audience as part of the play.

❖　　　❖　　　❖

Hecklers:
The Gallics had an interesting way of discouraging hecklers at an assembly. Should a man disturb the speaker, a soldier would approach him with a drawn sword and warn him to be quiet. If the heckler persisted, he would be threatened once more. But on the third interruption, the soldier would approach and cut the hecklers clothes to ribbons.

❖　　　❖　　　❖

Art:
The ancient Egyptians painted to a prescribed pattern. They were forbidden to make any changes to the set style of painting or sculpting and could not change the appearance of humans or indeed anything originating from nature, nor were they allowed to make the human form look more lifelike.

❖　　　❖　　　❖

Games:
A variety of games enjoyed a lot of popularity in Roman times. Not satisfied to just play the games for the sake of amusement, many Romans attempted to heighten their enjoyment by placing bets on the outcome of these games. Gambling became highly addictive and fearing for the well-being of their subjects, the forum passed laws banning all games of chance with one exception. Chess was the only game exempt, as the moves were made not by the roll of a dice, but by the skill of the player.

7. Law, Order and Authority

Crime:

The criminal classes of Kara-jang, a medieval eastern kingdom, would carry poison with them when setting out to commit particularly heinous crimes. The intent was to commit suicide should they be caught and so avoid the torture to which they would otherwise be subjected if convicted. The authorities, being wise to this trick, would always carry dog dung with them when on duty. Should they catch a criminal who had swallowed some poison, they would force him to eat the dung. This would induce him to vomit up the poison, save his life, and ensure that he was answerable for his crimes.

❖　　　❖　　　❖

Medieval England was plagued with bands of marauding thieves and villains. This problem was so endemic that a law was passed demanding that hedges be cleared from roadsides to an extent of two hundred feet on either side. As a further precaution, ditches were also filled to avoid unexpected ambushes.

❖　　　❖　　　❖

Theft was a problem in ancient Egypt despite the draconian punishments associated with the crime. In an attempt to curb the resulting disruption caused by thieving, a concession was granted to the thieves. All professional thieves were required to register their names with the chief of police. Subsequently, each time they performed a robbery they had to inform the chief of their crime, detailing what they took, where and when. The victim would then go to the police and request the recovery of his goods. Again, he would detail all that had been taken together with other particulars of the crime which would allow the police to identify the thief. The victim then paid one quarter the value of the goods taken and the items would be restored to him undamaged. The chief of police retained a cut of this money and gave the rest to the thief.

❖   ❖   ❖

Criminals:

Criminals convicted by the Leucadians, an ancient Ionian island people, could be chosen to participate in a sacrifice performed annually to avert evil. The criminal would have to suffer being thrown from a certain rocky cliff, but wishing to give the criminal a chance of survival he would first have a great many birds fastened to him so that their fluttering would break his fall. Of course, he would ultimately end up in the sea, but the Leucadians would have a number of fishing boats on stand by waiting to rescue the criminal. Once they made sure he was all right, he would be taken to safety in exile.

❖   ❖   ❖

At one time the Ethiopians invaded Egypt. They considered it best to colonise the land in an attempt to retain possession. Subsequently any Ethiopian found breaking the law would have their nose cut off and they would then be settled in Egypt. The authorities assumed that the wrongdoer would be so ashamed of their appearance they would not dare break the law again and would instead become a benefit to society.

❖   ❖   ❖

Punishment:

Murder was considered the worst of crimes in ancient Egypt. Indeed so seriously was it regarded that anyone even accidentally witnessing a murder without trying to prevent it, was considered an accessory and punished as severely as the perpetrator.

❖   ❖   ❖

An Egyptian who witnessed a robbery was obliged to attempt to arrest the thief or to at least provide information leading to his arrest. Failure to do so would result in the witness being condemned to a whipping and incarceration for three days without food.

❖   ❖   ❖

Capital punishment did not exist in the laws of medieval Ireland. However serious a crime, a fine would always be exacted. Nevertheless, kings always claimed the right to enact their own laws and would in fact pass the sentence of death for certain offences. These crimes varied greatly by modern day notions of severity. For instance, the death penalty was imposed on anyone lighting a fire before the Pascal fire was lit on the Hill of Tara. On the other hand, a sentence of death would be passed down to anyone convicted of murdering someone attending a fair meeting.

❖   ❖   ❖

A non-judicial sentence could be passed to a person who had accidentally killed another in ancient Ireland. This sentence entailed casting the killer adrift in a rudderless boat with no sail or oars. The person owning the stretch of shoreline where this boat came ashore would have the right to detain the passenger. The landowner could then stipulate a fine for his release.

❖   ❖   ❖

Assault:
The monks of medieval England were not above a little conflict with each other and indeed the public in general. The problem reached such a level that mendicant laws were enforced prohibiting the friars from assaulting each other with stones (or anything else coming to hand) or from mutilating the lay-folk.

❖   ❖   ❖

Compensation:

According to Brehon Law certain sums were set out as standard fees of compensation should a man suffer bodily injury by another. The law attached a specific amount of compensation to each part of the body. Some of these were straight forward enough, but some a little bizarre. For instance, if a man's left testicle were cut off he would be entitled to maximum compensation. Conversely, having the right testicle removed would only bring a small sum in compensation. This was because it was believed that the left testicle stored the means needed to give life whereas the right was little more than ornamental. Furthermore, a clergyman incurring an injury of this nature to either testicle could receive no more than the minimum compensation as he was expected not to have need of his reproductive organs.

There were various means by which an injured party could recover the compensation awarded to him by an Irish court should the defendant fail to pay. One such method entitled the plaintiff to seize certain goods or cattle to the value of the fine. These would be held in ransom for a certain period giving the debtor a chance to settle his dues. If he still failed to do so, the creditor would, with witnesses, sell the good. Any expenses incurred would be removed from the sale price along with the value of the fine and any excess returned to the debtor.

An unusual means by which a creditor in medieval Ireland could recover his debt entailed him undergoing a fast. Having given due notice of his intentions, the injured party would arrive at the home of the debtor and sitting on the doorstep, would begin the fast. At this point, the debtor was obliged to also partake in the fast. It was considered extremely shameful for him to either refuse to submit to or break the fast as he could incur a total loss of character, this being an unendurable state in Ireland at that time. The fast would be maintained until settlement, or a promise of settlement, was made.

Laws:

Various laws were set down over the years among different civilisations. A selection of these are given as follows:

Infanticide – Parents who killed their children would be given an unusual punishment. They were required to stand with the dead body in their arms for three days and nights under supervision. It was thought that as the parent gave life to the child they should not be given a very harsh punishment. This was not the case however if the offspring killed a parent. In these cases, the punishment was extreme. First, they would have strips the size of a finger cut from their flesh by a sharp reed. Then they would be put onto a bed of reeds and burnt alive. So conversely, the harshness of their punishment reflected the fact that they killed the person who had given them life.

Rape and adultery – A man raping a married woman was given the deterring punishment of castration. However a man committing adultery would not be as drastically penalised, he would be given a thousand blows of a rod. In cases of adultery in fact, the woman came off worse, as she would have her nose cut off. This was a preventative measure against further straying as it was considered that a woman enticed a man by her shapeliest feature – her nose!

War – Women of ancient Ireland were exempt by law from taking part in wars.

Sentencing – The medieval Sri Lankan people the Taprobane, had neither lawsuits nor law courts. However, their elected king was assigned thirty advisers by his people. These advisers also acted as jury to their countrymen. Any wrongdoer would have to put their case before these advisers and in the worst possible scenario if convicted as guilty, could be condemned to death. However, this sentence would only stand if a majority voted the same way. But all was not lost for the condemned. There was always a right of appeal where a jury of seventy would then be appointed. If these seventy then acquitted the accused, the original jury of thirty would be held in the deepest disgrace. Should the king be guilty of a major wrongdoing, he too in principle could be condemned to death. However no one would actually carry out the sentence, instead his people would boycott him and refuse to speak to him.

Discoveries – The Indians had a law which stated that anyone discovering something that proved deadly would be put to death unless he also found a cure. However, should a cure be found then the discoverer would be fated and rewarded by the king.

Debts – The Indians had an effective method of dealing with debtors. If a debtor failed to pay his creditor and continued to put him off to avoid payment, he could be subjected to an unusual law. If the creditor could get physically close to the debtor, he would draw a circle on the ground around him. The debtor was then bound by law to remain in the circle until he made immediate arrangements to pay what he owed. Should he leave the circle before the debt was settled, he would incur the penalty of death.

Law-making – The philosophers of India were permitted to draw-up laws. When these were made public, they were judged for their ability to bring prosperity to the land. Those philosophers whose ideas were found unworkable on three occasions were required by law to remain silent for life, whereas those found correct were declared exempt from paying tax.

❖   ❖   ❖

Court System:

Lawsuits reached epidemic proportions in ancient Rome. The litigious population brought so much litigation to the system that additional courtrooms had to be built to cope with the demand.

❖   ❖   ❖

Roman lawyers would hire a mob to act as claqueurs and sit in court while they debated a case. The function of the claqueurs was to cheer and clap all utterances from the lawyer hiring them in an attempt to both impress the judge and jury, heighten the lawyer's reputation and to put off the opposition.

❖   ❖   ❖

The ancient Irish court system was such that a husband and wife were permitted to give evidence against one another. However, a daughter was barred from giving evidence against her father no matter what accusations he brought against her. Evidence could only be heard from a man if he had reached the age of seventeen or had begun to grow a beard.

❖   ❖   ❖

Judges:
Egyptian judges were always well paid so they would have enough personal money to be able to resist the temptation of bribery.

❖   ❖   ❖

Under Brehon law, medieval Irish judges were entitled to a cut of one-twelfth of the fine they imposed as a payment for their judgement.

❖   ❖   ❖

It was believed that a divine power watched over Irish judges. For this reason if a judge were to deviate from the truth, red blotches were thought to manifest on his cheek. If however he were to give a false judgement that was later discovered, he would be personally liable for damages.

❖   ❖   ❖

Lawyers:

Roman law stipulated that for a court case to be valid, the lawyers had to present the case before noon.

❖   ❖   ❖

Lawsuits:

The Musicanus, ancient inhabitants of the Indus Valley, gave very careful consideration to those with whom they made a contract and would only do business with people they absolutely trusted. This was because there was no redress should a contract be broken as the authorities had a policy of not allowing their courts to be filled with these types of lawsuits.

❖   ❖   ❖

Trials:

Medieval trials required the plaintive to undergo specific ordeals which would indicate the innocence or trustworthiness of the person testifying. Different trials were used in different parts of Europe and could involve water or heat. The ordeal by water required the accused to fast and attend church to swear his innocence on holy relics. Then, at the location of his ordeal, he would drink specially blessed water before being thrown into a pond or stream. Supposedly, the innocent would sink while the guilty floated. The ordeal by heat on the other hand required the accused to either grasp a hot iron or fish pebbles by hand out of a cauldron of boiling water. The accused hands would subsequently be bandaged but if a few days later the hands showed no sign of injury, the person was considered innocent. Anticipating this outcome, those about to undergo this particular trial would safeguard themselves by applying a salve of egg whites and wild radishes to their hands. Once dry, this salve offered some protection to the participants.

❖   ❖   ❖

The ancient Irish had a system of trials or ordeals to which they would subject the accused and thereby ascertain innocence or guilt. One ordeal involved heating a piece of metal in a fire of blackthorn or rowan until red-hot. The accused's tongue would be made to pass over this heated metal which was believed to burn the person telling lies, but leave the innocent unscathed. Another ordeal required the accused to thrust his hand into a bucket filled with bog dust and charcoal and to pick one of three stones buried there. The stones placed in the bucket where white, black or speckled. If the black stone was selected, then the accused was deemed guilty; if the white stone was drawn, he was innocent; and the speckled one implied he was half guilty.

❖   ❖   ❖

Land Ownership:
The Dalmatians of the eastern Mediterranean had a fair system of land ownership. Land was distributed between the people every seven years. At the end of this period, each allocation would be given back to be redistributed again. This way everyone had an opportunity of cultivating rich land as well as barren.

❖   ❖   ❖

Spartan law declared that no citizen should possess more land than another and that each should have an equal share of any public land available. To ensure that there would be no jealousy among the citizens over any possessions, they took care to advocate that money should be held in very low esteem. As a result, no one was driven by financial gain.

❖   ❖   ❖

Egyptian land was divided into sectors of equal size and rented out. If, after the Nile flooded, any farmer's plot was carried away, surveyors would come to determine by how much the land had reduced and would offer an appropriately discounted rent. It is believed that by this means the Egyptians mastered geometry.

❖   ❖   ❖

A tribe of barbarians from ancient Italy found it necessary to relieve their land of some of its population in times of need when food was scarce. As they considered killing their children a most heinous crime they had to resort to banishment. All youths born during a prescribed year were sent off to colonise another area. Before leaving these young people would participate in a ceremony in which their tribe begged for forgiveness for imposing this banishment.

❖   ❖   ❖

The law of ancient Ireland dictated that clan land should be divided equally amongst all adult men. When one of these landowners died, this estate could not be passed to his heir. Instead, the land had to be returned to the chief who would redistribute it in its entirety once more.

❖   ❖   ❖

Measurements:

The ancient Irish had various means of measuring lengths and distances. As other societies, some of these were based on physical entities, the length of a grain of wheat for instance being the smallest measure. Some measurements however were a little less tangible as they were indicated by sound. One such measure was the distance travelled by the sound of a small hand bell. The distance over which a barn door cock could be heard reckoned another measure of length. The ancient Germans also used this measure.

❖   ❖   ❖

The amount of land an ancient Irish person could have around his home was legally determined by his rank in society. The unit of measurement used to allocate this land was based on the distance a man could cast a spear while standing at the house.

❖   ❖   ❖

Property:
European medieval kings acquired property from all manner of sources. For example, the king could exercise his right to claim the property of bastards or strangers dying on his territory. He could also claim as lost property anything that wandered away from its owner.

❖   ❖   ❖

The king of the oriental kingdom of Manzi liked to see all his subjects well provided for. When out riding, if he saw a poor man's house dwarfed by the houses of rich neighbours, he would make orders to ensure the smaller home be built up to equal those around it.

❖   ❖   ❖

The Iberian Cantabrarian women were highly regarded in their society and daughters were named as heirs to property.

❖   ❖   ❖

The Irish occasionally used fences to mark their territory. Although a law existed which stipulated how to construct a fence and how long it should take, the law was not enforced. However, if a lawsuit was brought against the man because the fence had injured another's cattle, then he would be prosecuted if it was shown he had flouted the law when building the fence.

❖   ❖   ❖

Ostracism:

The ancient Greeks had a humbling method of preventing those in power ever becoming too caught up in their own worth and prestige. They imposed a sentence of ostracism on the ruling classes whereby citizens would cast votes for the leaders they wished to see banished. The votes would be counted in the market place and the man with the most votes cast against him would be banished for a period of ten years. However, to avoid apathy amongst the voters, if the total number of votes cast numbered less than six thousand then the whole exercise was voided.

❖   ❖   ❖

Employment:

Those in local authority in Egypt kept careful watch over the occupations of their citizens as no one was permitted to lead an idle life and so be a bad example to the community. The magistrates would prescribe certain dates when each person was expected to present themselves to state their name, address and occupation. These details would be recorded and used to monitor the people.

❖   ❖   ❖

Prostitutes:

The suburbs of Khan-balik, a city of the medieval province of Cathay, was said to be home to a great number of prostitutes. When a dignitary visited the city, a succession of prostitutes was offered to him and his retinue by the city officials for as long as the visitors remained in the city. The prostitutes were given no payment, instead this service to their city was considered as fulfilment of their tax dues which saved the taxman from attempting to otherwise calculate the amount due!

❖   ❖   ❖

Women:

Roman women had a guardian appointed to them. This could be her father, or another of his male relations, while she remained single, or her husband after marriage. A woman was only exempt from having a guardian if she was the mother of three children. Indeed being the mother of three entitled Roman woman to all manner of freedoms otherwise denied to her. This rule was passed in an attempt to encourage women to increase the birth-rate.

❖   ❖   ❖

Medieval women were subject to a great deal of misogyny, particularly from the respected scholars of the day. Different beliefs concerning women abounded, the majority of which denounced all womankind. For instance, the Gnostics held the belief that the created world was inferior to spiritual reality. Following this line of thought, if matter was evil then to create matter was to create evil. And as woman were responsible for procreation, it naturally followed that woman were evil. It was not just the Gnostics that held this view. Both Saints Jerome and Augustine held the view that woman and marriage were to be looked down on. Jerome went so far as to declare marriage as a venial sin, redeemed only by the creation of children.

❖   ❖   ❖

Irish women of medieval times were held in high regard by society. They held respected positions as judges, lawyers and physicians.

❖   ❖   ❖

Metal:

Iron was held in esteem by many societies. The Romans attributed magical properties to it and when founding new colonies, they traced its circuit with an iron ploughshare. Likewise, certain bridges would only be repaired using iron.

98

Roman witches were believed to gather their magical herbs at midnight using bronze implements.

❖ ❖ ❖

Monarchy:
The Persians believed that monarchs were in a class of their own when it came to ethics. They believed that they could not help having the vices of envy and pride. Envy may seem an unusual vice for a monarch but according to Persian logic, it is a natural human weakness and is therefore unavoidable. Pride resulted from the power and wealth possessed by the monarchs, which in turn lead to an assumption that they were better than anyone else.

❖ ❖ ❖

The Taprobane, a medieval people living in what is now Sri Lanka, neither slept beyond dawn nor took a siesta. They also had no lawsuits or law courts. Of particular interest was their choice of monarch. The people elected the king from a selection of men who were both elderly and childless. Should the king become a father during his reign, he was forced to abdicate so preventing the monarchy from becoming hereditary.

❖ ❖ ❖

According to an Ethiopian custom, should any of their kings be maimed in any way, then his closest associate would have to suffer the same fate and this rule was enforced even if the king died. Due to this custom, the kings tended to be very well cared for and closely guarded from harm.

❖ ❖ ❖

The southern Arabian Sabaean kings were said to live in effeminate luxury and held absolute authority. However, because of an old prophecy, they were not permitted to leave their palace. Should one do so he would be stoned to death on the spot.

The care of medieval Indian kings was in the hands of women who were allowed inside the palace whereas the bodyguards remained stationed outside the palace gates. However should a woman kill the king she was rewarded by being allowed to consort with his successor. Because of the many plots planned against him, the king would not sleep during the day and at night would continually change beds.

❖   ❖   ❖

Ethiopian kings were not allowed to put any of his subjects to death, even if he had bestowed a death sentence on a civilian following a trial. In these cases, a messenger would be sent to the condemned man telling him of his fate. The man would then be obliged to carry out his own sentence and kill himself.

❖   ❖   ❖

The ancient Irish had two specific criteria for the election of candidates for the position of king or ruling chief. Both the father and grandfather of the candidate must have been of noble stock; and he must be free from any blemish or deformity. The latter stipulation was designed to ensure that the ruler chosen would have no obstacle in his ability to rule efficiently or any impediment to lessen his subjects' respect.

❖   ❖   ❖

The ancient Irish believed there were certain signs of aristocracy in a person. These were an oval face, fair hair and skin, white delicate hands and slender tapering fingers.

❖   ❖   ❖

The high kings of Ireland had certain restrictions or prohibitions imposed upon them. Some were no more than sensible precautions against harm whereas others were intended as safeguards against bad luck. For instance the king was forbidden to allow the sun to rise on him while he was still in bed, in other words he had to get up before sunrise. He could not alight from his carriage in a certain district on a Wednesday. And most importantly, he could not, under any circumstance, travel anti-clockwise around Leinster.

❖   ❖   ❖

Public Office:
The chief magistrate of Platae in ancient Greece had to uphold certain customs while he held office. He was forbidden to touch iron and, other than for very special ceremonies, could only wear white clothes.

❖   ❖   ❖

Rich citizens of Rhodes were appointed on a rotational basis to public office. The appointments were made according to the wealth of the citizen, as once in office, they were responsible for personally paying for all expenses connected with their office.

❖   ❖   ❖

As a mark of respect, Egyptians coming before a magistrate or other official would place a hand over their mouth to prevent their breath from contacting the officials' face.

❖   ❖   ❖

Politics:
The ancient British had a law forbidding politics to be discussed anywhere but in the public assembly. This law was set to protect ignorant people from being alarmed by false gossip.

❖   ❖   ❖

Passport:
The Egyptians used a system of passports not too unlike those used today. These passports would contain a physical description of

the holder together with details of his trade or occupation. The holder would then be required to show this document when leaving his district and again when entering another. Recording false statements on this documentation was a capital offence as the Egyptian class system was rigidly adhered to and social climbing not permitted.

❖　　❖　　❖

The Egyptians passport system was extended to the dead as well as to the living. This last passport reported all the confessional deeds of the dead person and was intended as the soul's passport to eternal happiness.

❖　　❖　　❖

Taxes:
The concept of taxes is not new, nor are punishments imposed on those dodging their obligations in this area. Egyptians had to make a written statement of their sources of income. Failure to do this would lead to a rather drastic penalty – death!

❖　　❖　　❖

Taxes were imposed on all manner of goods in the orient. However, the authorities would waive the taxes due on livestock if lightning struck any animal belonging to a farmer. Indeed the taxes would be waived for three years as it was considered bad luck for lightening to strike any man's possessions. This extended to the merchandise of any ship, normally also due for taxation. This leniency was exhibited because it was thought that God must have been angry to have let loose the lightning and so it would be bad luck to have any money from these goods in the treasury.

❖　　❖　　❖

The Tartars of northern Asia would never levy a tax on the property of a dead man as they considered this bad luck.

❖   ❖   ❖

Guards:
Egyptian slaves forced to work in mines were guarded by foreign soldiers to ensure no compassion would be felt by the guards towards their captives. With the lack of a common language, no conversation could be struck up between the slaves and their guards, which prevented the possibility of friendship and sympathetic aid.

❖   ❖   ❖

8. Animals and the Environment

Pets:

It is widely known that the ancient Egyptians had a very high regard for their cats. In fact, they loved them so much that when one died, its owner, together with the rest of the household, would go into mourning. They displayed their grief for all the world to see by shaving off their eyebrows. Whatever their regard for their cats however, the Egyptians took more drastic measures when their dog died. On the death of a dog, the whole household would shave their entire bodies, including their heads!

❖   ❖   ❖

The Egyptians used to bring a favourite cat with them while out hunting. The cat would work as a retriever whenever its owner killed anything.

❖   ❖   ❖

Dogs:

The Romans were given advice on how to stop their dogs from running away. The procedure involved measuring the length of the dog's tail with a rod, then smearing this rod with butter and allowing the dog to lick it off.

❖   ❖   ❖

It was believed that a dog could be silenced if it were to stand in the shadow of a hyena which was cast by a full moon.

❖   ❖   ❖

Indian dogs were said to be so brave that once they got hold of their prey they refused to let go unless water was poured down their nostrils. Sometimes they bit their unfortunate victim with such vigour, their eyes were said to fall out.

❖   ❖   ❖

Pigs:
The Egyptians used pigs to trample seeds into the ground after sowing thus avoiding the necessity of doing the job with a harrow.

❖   ❖   ❖

Those imbibing sow's milk were thought to become infected by leprosy.

❖   ❖   ❖

Sheep:
Apparently the sheep in Arabia had such long tails that they trailed on the ground as they walked. So to stop their tails getting sores from friction against the road, the shepherds had the ingenious idea of making little carts for their tails so that they could trundle them along without touching the ground.

❖   ❖   ❖

The Romans protected the wool on their sheep by tying skins around the animals. This ensured fleeces with particularly fine wool.

❖   ❖   ❖

The Greeks, Romans and Egyptians utilised a monetary system common to that used now, employing precious metals for their coinage. However, this coinage could be freely substituted with sheep, which in turn were equated with fixed amounts of other goods.

Goats:

The Egyptians would at times use goats and other animals when praying and would ask their gods to transfer any misfortune about to befall an Egyptian citizen onto the head of the goats. For this reason no Egyptian would eat the head of an animal. The Jews had a similar ritual where they would bring two goats before their altar. They would then cast lots on behalf of the goat, assigning one to the Lord and the other to receive all the sins of the people. This latter goat, named as the 'scapegoat' would then be brought out into the desert.

❖   ❖   ❖

The goat was thought by the Roman Aeolian to have the ability to breath through its ears as well as its nostrils.

❖   ❖   ❖

Bears:

Aristotle observed the hibernation habits of bears and decided the reason a bear could survive forty days without any kind of nourishment was due to its intestines. He believed a bear's intestines had the ability to wrinkle and compress during hibernation meaning the bear would not get hungry. On waking from its sleep the bear would immediately eat a plant called cuckoo-pint which would induce flatulence. The build up of internal gas would open out the gut once more and allow the bear to eat.

❖   ❖   ❖

The Romans thought that a bear gave birth to a shapeless lump of flesh. This lump would be formed into the likeness of a bear by being licked into shape by its mother.

❖   ❖   ❖

Horses:

A horse that swished its tail whilst being ridden was considered unsightly by the medieval Far Eastern people, the Kara-jangians. To overcome this apparent problem they would remove a couple of joints from the horses tail bone to prevent it from swinging too much.

❖   ❖   ❖

Wolves were thought to hold certain powers over horses. For instance, it was thought that if a horse trod on the footprint of a wolf it would become numb and unable to move. Likewise, anatomical parts of a wolf were also thought to induce paralysis in horses. The vertebra of a wolf thrown into the path of a four horse team was believed to stop the horses in their tracks.

❖   ❖   ❖

A mare was thought to miscarry if it were to smell the wick of an extinguished lamp for a prolonged period.

❖   ❖   ❖

Donkeys:

According to the ancient writer Aeolian, a donkey would not bray if a stone were hung from its tail.

❖   ❖   ❖

Bulls:

At any given time, the Egyptians had a sacred bull inhabiting their temple at Memphis. Amongst other duties, this bull was used as an oracle. Anyone with a query would approach the bull with a gift of food in their hand. If the bull accepted the food, then the answer was positive, however if the food was refused, it was considered as a bad omen. This gift of prophecy possessed by the bull, could also be transposed to others. Children that smelled his breath were also given the power of prophecy.

A supposedly effective method for stopping a charging bull was to tie a scarf around the right knee and squarely face the charging bull.

❖ ❖ ❖

Cows:

The cows of the ancient Persian city of Susa were hard working, drawing one hundred buckets of water each a day. However apparently they always stopped working when they reached the hundredth bucket no matter how much they were encouraged to continue working. The locals believed they could count.

❖ ❖ ❖

The ancient Irish thought their cattle would succumb to disease if they had eaten a particular variety of caterpillar. This disease could only be cured if the cattle in question were made drink water in which an amulet shaped like the caterpillar had been soaked.

❖ ❖ ❖

Each year at the beginning of May, ancient Irish druids would drive cattle between two fires while offering incantations. This was believed to protect the cows for the duration of the following year.

❖ ❖ ❖

Ants:

The lees remaining from pressing olives for their oil was used to coat the floors of the threshing sheds, as it was believed to keep away ants.

❖ ❖ ❖

Ants were believed to possess certain human characteristics. It was thought that they buried their dead in the empty husks of wheat in the same way that man would use a coffin.

❖   ❖   ❖

Scorpions:
Due to the abundance of scorpions in Libya, the natives would protect themselves while asleep by smearing the feet of their beds with garlic.

❖   ❖   ❖

Snakes:
Snakes could be induced to leave their dens if the feathers from a vulture were burned in their vicinity.

❖   ❖   ❖

Eggs:
Methods of incubating eggs go back to Egyptian times. Ovens were specially built for the process which involved collecting the eggs and placing them on bran-strewn mats within large ovens. Light was admitted into the ovens, either through windows or from a lamp. Fires were lit in the ovens twice a day and allowed to burn away. The eggs were arranged in lines above these fires and were regularly moved across the lines to ensure they received equal amounts of warmth. After six days, each egg would be examined to see if the chicks were still alive within the eggs. The heating, rotation and inspection of the eggs continued for a prescribed time until their expected hatch date arrived. The rearers would continue to inspect the eggs for signs of life by holding each to their eyelid. If it felt warm against the skin, then the chick was alive.

❖   ❖   ❖

The Romans thought eggs could be addled by thunder or even by being within the range of a hawk's call. To avoid the eggs spoiling a safeguard was employed whereby an iron nail would be placed beneath the straw the eggs rested upon. Equally effective was said to be a clod of earth turned up by a plough. Again, this needed to be placed beneath the eggs for effectiveness.

❖   ❖   ❖

There was a belief that cockroaches ate swallows' eggs. However, to overcome the cockroach's appetite and protect her young, the mother swallow had a ruse. She would cover the eggs with celery leaves and the cockroaches would stay away.

❖   ❖   ❖

Ring-tail doves were believed to protect their eggs from sorcery by incorporating bay leaves into their nests.

❖   ❖   ❖

Fertility:
Druids believed that giving a barren animal a drink containing mistletoe would make it fertile.

❖   ❖   ❖

It was believed that no male vultures were ever born. As the bird realised this, and did not wish to face extinction, they had to devise an alternative method to ensure reproduction. To impregnate themselves they would fly up into the air and open their beaks towards the east wind. The rush of air entering their body was believed to impregnate them. It was then thought that the birds had to endure a gestation period of three years before their eggs appeared.

❖   ❖   ❖

Protection:
Tibetan travellers protected their animals from marauding wild life by throwing giant green canes onto their camp fire. These canes would swell with the heat until they eventually burst with a loud bang. This bang would scare away potential predators. To stop their own animals from being alarmed at the commotion should they not be used to the noise, the travellers would block up the animals' ears for the night.

❖   ❖   ❖

Appetite:
An animal's appetite could apparently be suppressed by tying a cord around the middle of its tail.

❖   ❖   ❖

Fish:
The Brahmans of India would cast spells over predatory fish to protect their pearl divers from attack. During the night, when the legal pearl fisherman did not dive, the spells would be lifted, allowing the fish to do as they pleased. This was also considered an effective method against thieves, as the illegal divers, who came out at night, would not be afforded any protection from the fish.

❖   ❖   ❖

An Egyptian religious regulation dictated that a fried fish should be eaten at the door of a house on a certain noted day of the year.

❖   ❖   ❖

A certain species of fish in the Nile were reputed to allow themselves to be caught by fisherman who sang to them.

❖   ❖   ❖

Spiders:
Tarantulas were said to infest houses in India. However, the Indians made use of their presence by using them as portents when brokering a deal. In fact both parties in the transaction would watch for these spiders as both needed a sign to understand if the deal struck was to be good or not. The noises the spiders made as they scuttled about would be listened out for during the meeting. The direction from which the noise came, whether to the left, right or above, gave the opposite party the information needed as to whether to continue with the deal or not.

❖   ❖   ❖

Flies:
It was believed that the flies of Pisa knew when the Olympic season was at hand and would leave the area for the duration of the games as a sign of peace towards the inhabitants and the visitors.

❖   ❖   ❖

The Romans thought they could revive a drowned fly by sprinkling ashes on it and leaving it in the sun.

❖   ❖   ❖

Insects:
It was believed that beetles could be killed by scattering roses on them.

❖   ❖   ❖

The Romans believed caterpillars could be eliminated from a garden if a young menstruating girl were to walk bare-foot three times around the garden in question with her hair and clothing loose. Another similar superstition related by Aeolian claimed that caterpillars could be killed if a menstruating woman walked through a vegetable patch in which they were eating.

Elephants:

Elephant fat was thought to possess magical properties. Not only would the fat cure poisoning from any savage creature, but also it was believed to protect a man from an animal attack if he were to rub it on himself.

❖　　　❖　　　❖

Earth:

The Hyperboreans, a tribe that were reported to live beyond the north wind, had the rather bizarre belief that the earth turned on enormous hinges!

❖　　　❖　　　❖

Kings and other aristocracy of India sat on the ground – the same as all their subjects. They rejected more regal seating arrangements as they considered the earth worthy of honour since humans both came from the earth and returned to it on death. They did not therefore wish to be seated higher than the earth.

❖　　　❖　　　❖

The Derbices of the Black Sea worshipped mother earth and would not sacrifice or eat anything female. So although, amongst other delicacies, they ate the old men of their society, the women were buried.

❖　　　❖　　　❖

The Brachmanes of India believed that the earth was formed when the creator dropped a seed into the water. The world then sprang from this seed.

❖　　　❖　　　❖

Rivers:

The Persians were an environmentally friendly bunch. They were very protective over the cleanliness of their waterways and would neither urinate or even wash in a river. In fact, they would not throw anything into a river that was dead or otherwise considered unclean.

❖   ❖   ❖

Farmers of ancient Greece were advised not to cross a river until they had offered up a prayer and then washed their hands in the water of the river.

❖   ❖   ❖

Floods:

The Nile was the life-blood of the people of Egypt who relied on it flooding each year. To measure the level of the Nile at any given time, the kings set up a Nilometer at Memphis which the local priests monitored. They would regularly gauge the level of the river and send out Nile forecasts to the surrounding cities.

❖   ❖   ❖

Weather:

It seems that the Irish weather was always a source of conversation. Apparently, in ancient times, the weather was widely reported to have been so cold in Ireland that the Irish endured a miserable existence.

❖   ❖   ❖

The peoples living on the borders of the Caucasian mountains were subject to heavy falls of snow. As a result, during the winter months, the people would carry staves with them so if they should be overcome by a snowstorm they could use the stave to push a breathing hole through the snow. This stave was also recognised as a signal: following a snowstorm any passer-by seeing one in the ground would dig up the snow and rescue the person buried beneath.

❖ ❖ ❖

The call of a crane was thought to bring on showery weather.

❖ ❖ ❖

The Nicaeans of southern Thrace believed they could foretell the weather by watching their ox. They believed that when an ox lay on its right side rain was threatened while if it lay on its left side, fine weather was to be expected. A storm could be expected if an ox ate copiously.

❖ ❖ ❖

Various animals were believed to have the ability to forecast the weather. For instance, a storm could be expected if sheep dug at the ground or goats huddled together or if an owl hooted softly. Violent winds could be expected if ducks were seen flapping their wings.

❖ ❖ ❖

The Greeks had little regard for the Scythian climate which they described as being four months of cold and eight months of winter. This is perhaps not a totally unexpected observance considering Scythia occupied a region around the Caucasus towards north-east Asia Minor and was believed by the ancient Greeks to be the home of the north wind.

❖ ❖ ❖

What a Difference a Day Makes:
Ancient civilisations each had their own methods of marking the passing of a day. The Babylonians measured a day's length as extending from sunrise to sunrise. Conversely, the Athenians

marked the interval between sunsets, as did the Celtic druids, while the Umbrians chose the period from midday to midday. Apparently, ordinary people saw a day as existing between dawn and dusk, whereas the Egyptians had a more modern outlook and measured a day from midnight to midnight.

❖   ❖   ❖

Time:

The Romans marked the day as consisting of twenty-four hours, which was in turn sub-divided into two equal parts. The night hours, i.e. sunset to sunrise, contained twelve hours, as did the daylight period, sunrise to sunset. However, this distribution resulted in summer daylight hours containing more time than the corresponding night hours. So for instance during midsummer's day, the daylight hours would each contain the equivalent of one and a quarter modern hours whereas the night time hour would comprise three-quarters of a modern hour.

❖   ❖   ❖

As a forerunner to the alarm clock, Romans had water clocks which were fitted with floats. By a clever arrangement, on striking the hour, pebbles or eggs would be tossed into the air from the clock.

❖   ❖   ❖

Sun:

The Atlas tribe of North Africa uttered terrible curses against the sun as it rose and set. They believed it to be the cause of all their problems, both personal and in their fields.

❖   ❖   ❖

The Ethiopians reviled the sun which they believed continuously waged war against them by burning both their bodies and the earth.

Stars:

The ancient Greeks believed that stars were composed of stone and emitted light through friction with the ether through which they travelled. They also believed that if these stars were to deviate from the path along which they travelled, they would come crashing down onto the earth. For instance, they believed that shooting stars were dislodged from their orbit when the ether surrounding them suddenly ignited, blasting them earthward. These stars were thought to land mainly in the sea.

❖   ❖   ❖

Earthquakes:

The Babylonians believed earthquakes were the result of action between the planets of Saturn, Jupiter and Mars, all of which exerted their force on the earth. Pliny the Elder, who reported this belief, had a more reasoned argument as to the cause of earthquakes. He believed them to be caused by the wind! His belief was based on a very logical observation. He noticed that just before an earthquake the sea was invariably calm and the sky so still and motionless that even birds couldn't fly. He attributed this to all the air which supported them having been taken away.

❖   ❖   ❖

Mankind:

The Egyptians believed that man was a creature of the marshes and swamp long before current thinking espoused the notion that we originally evolved from the sea. But the Egyptians were not evolutionists; they came to this conclusion because of the smoothness of man's skin and the fact that he favoured a wet rather than a solely dry diet.

❖   ❖   ❖

Monuments:

The Egyptians were thought to be able to both raise and sustain a large population and build such fine monuments because of the extreme cheapness of raising a child. This was calculated as being just twenty drachmas from infancy to maturity per child. The weather helped, as due to the warmness of the climate the children did not need shoes or much clothing. The children were not fussy eaters either, it was reported that they would eat anything that came to hand.

❖   ❖   ❖

Trees:

The Jews living in ancient Egypt were instructed not to cut down any fruit trees for wood during battle, believing that it was wrong to use any tree that could sustain life.

❖   ❖   ❖

Oriental soothsayers said that anyone planting trees would be blessed with long life.

❖   ❖   ❖

The oak tree was revered in Dodona, an ancient Greek sanctuary, as it was considered to be the first tree created, as well as being a useful source of food.

❖   ❖   ❖

Oil:

Babylonia reportedly produced great quantities of asphalt which they used, among other applications, to waterproof boats and construct buildings. Babylonia also produced a liquid form of this substance which they called naphtha. It was noted that this substance was very flammable and impossible to extinguish with water, which appeared to fan the flames. Instead, these fires were quenched with mud, vinegar, potash alum and bird-lime.

❖   ❖   ❖

Almanac:

The Greeks were advised to perform certain tasks on certain days of the month considered the best for the task at hand. So, sheep ought be sheared on the eleventh of a month whereas corn should be reaped on the twelfth. Sowing was to be avoided on the thirteenth although this was a good day for transplanting plants. The seventeenth was particularly good for making furniture or building ships.

❖   ❖   ❖

Egyptians believed that antelope were the first to be aware of the important time of year when Sirius, the Dog Star, was due to rise. The antelope would notify the Egyptians of the star's rising by sneezing.

❖   ❖   ❖

9. An Easy Mistake to Make!

In some instances the more bizarre customs and traditions of some nations, as reported by ancient geographers and historians, can nowadays be easily explained. Their take on the lifestyles they reported shows at times how easily certain traits could be misinterpreted and at other times how readily conclusions were arrived at which served to show neighbouring nations as strange in the extreme. The following illustrate some classic instances:

❖ ❖ ❖

The Natural World:

Strabo commented on the people of the ancient Greek city state Carystus, who combed and wove stones which were manufactured into towels. Strabo remarked that unlike linen towels which were cleaned by washing, these towels were cleaned by being placed into a fire. The stone that could produce fibre and withstand fire was of course asbestos.

❖ ❖ ❖

The gold of the Phtheirophagi, an ancient tribe living near the Black Sea, was not found by mining, instead it was said to issue down mountainsides in torrents. The tribe then collected the gold by laying fleeces into the water which would trap the gold as it coursed down the slope. Strabo concluded that this method of collecting gold must have given rise to the popular legend of Jason and the golden fleece.

❖ ❖ ❖

There was a suggestion in ancient times that land, which was porous, was subject to earthquakes. This porosity was due, in turn, to high humidity which caused fissures in the earth.

❖ ❖ ❖

Travellers to India reported with wonder trees that produced wool. This tree growing wool could be used as standard wool once the seeds had been removed. This wool was in fact cotton.

❖   ❖   ❖

The Libyans described a phenomenon whereby on occasion strange shapes could be seen gathering in the sky and these would take on the appearance of all kinds of animals. These shapes would sometimes be motionless and at other times move around. Sometimes they retreated from man and other times they would pursue. Their enormous size would strike terror in the beholder and on the occasions when these shapes overtook a person enveloping him in its midst, they would cause fear and a shivering sensation. These shapes were nothing more alarming than clouds, and when on the ground, fog.

❖   ❖   ❖

Strange Men:

Ctesias in his travels reported to the ancient world of the existence of Indian men who possessed only one large foot that they used to stand about on all day. This transpires to be nothing more than the holy men of the region who tended to stand about for long periods of time and although they were in possession of two perfectly good legs, they preferred standing on just one while tucking the other up under themselves.

❖   ❖   ❖

Beasts:

Marco Polo is famous for his adventures in little known lands and reported sightings of many strange beasts unseen in his native Venice. One such beast was described as a wild boar of monstrous size, as big as a buffalo, with huge tusks. Considering the location of these reports, it seems as though Marco Polo was actually looking at a hippopotamus.

Diodorus of Sicily reported on a strange breed of beast living in Arabia that was a cross between a camel and a leopard. The animal being described was in fact a giraffe.

❖ ❖ ❖

Prospecting Ants:

Several classical writers documented the existence of gold-digging ants in India. These 'ants' were said to dig up mounds of earth during the winter which contained gold dust. Tribesmen would try to take these mounds by stealth as the 'ants' would give chase and fight anyone they found stealing their mounds. It is now known that these ants are actually a species of small animal, still extant in certain parts of India. However, their gold-digging days have now come to an end!

❖ ❖ ❖

Cranes:

The ancients observed and attempted to rationalise natural occurrences. They would use logic to explain the behaviour of a range of animals and birds, such as for instance the crane. When cranes flew to a foreign land, they would stop to rest by a watering hole. It was thought that to protect the flock while they slept, two or three cranes would be selected to stand guard over the rest. To prevent the sentry birds from nodding off, these cranes would hold up a stone in one of their claws. Should they begin to slumber, they would loosen their grip on the stone. The sound of the falling stone splashing into the water would reawaken the crane. It was believed that this is why some cranes stood around on one leg.

❖ ❖ ❖

References

A Social History of Ancient Ireland, *The Gresham Publishing Co.*, P. W. Joyce

Aelion: On the Characteristics of Animals, *Loeb Classical Library*. Translated by A. F. Scholfield

Celsus: De Medicina, *Loeb Classical Library*. Translated by W. G. Spencer

Daily Life in Ancient Rome, *George Rutledge & Sons Ltd*, J. Carcopino

Diocese of Meath, Ancient and Modern, *Four Courts Press*, A. Cogan

Diodorus of Sicily, *Loeb Classical Library*. Translated by C. H. Oldfather

Dionysus of Halicarnasus: Roman Antiquities, *Loeb Classical Library*. Translated by E. Cary

Epictetus: The Golden Sayings, *P. F. Collier & Son*, Translated by Hastings Crossley

Everyday Things in Ancient Greece, *B. T. Batsford Ltd*, M. & C. Quennell

Greek and Roman Folklore, *Cooper SQ Publishers Inc*, W. R. Halliday

Herodotus; The Histories, *Penguin Classics*. Translated by Aubrey de Selincourt

Hesiod; Works and Days, *John Hopkins University Press*. Translated by A. N. Athanassikis

Hippocrates; On Airs, Water and Places, *Loeb Classical Library*. Translated by F. Adams

Julius Caesar; The Conquest of Gaul, *Penguin Classics*. Translated by J. A. Handford

Manetho; History of Egypt, *Loeb Classical Library*. Translated by W. G. Waddell

Marco Polo; The Travels, *Penguin Classics*. Translated by R. E. Latham

Plutarch; On Sparta, *Penguin Classics*. Translated by R. J. A. Talbert

Plutarch; The Rise and Fall of Athens, *Penguin Classics*. Translated by Ian Scott-Kilvert

Polybius; The Histories, *Loeb Classical Library*. Translated by H. L. Jones

Ptolomy: Tetrabiblos, *Loeb Classical Library*. Translated by F. G. Robbins

Sex and Marriage in Ancient Ireland, *Mercier Press*, P. Power

Strabo; The Geography of Strabo, *Loeb Classical Library*. Translated by H. L. Jones

Tacitus; On Britain and Rome, *Penguin Classics*. Translated by H. Mattingly

The Ancient Egyptians; Their Life and Customs, *Senate*. J. Gardner Wilkinson

The Holy Bible, *Oxford University Press*, The King James version

The Medieval Vision, *Oxford University Press*, Carolly Erickson

The Pelican History of Greece, *Pelican Books*, A. R. Burn.

Index